Beware the Snap of a Twig

James McNally

Michael Terence Publishing

First published in paperback by
Michael Terence Publishing in 2020
www.mtp.agency

ISBN 9781913653842

Cover image
by permission of Eric Ziolo,
Maire de Bort-les-Orgues

Cover design

Beware the Snap of a Twig

During and since the war the work of the "Résistance" and of the "Maquis" has inspired numberless pens. Fecund imaginations have thrilled the world with romantic and breath-taking stories of underground activities in enemy-occupied Europe. Heroes whose mission it was to land in these countries and organise the patriots' work have given colourful and thrilling accounts of their activities and adventures. This is not a general treatise on the resistance movement. It is a narrative, without literary pretensions, of things seen and experienced in France from 1940 until V-E day, a simple and exact description of the atmosphere in which the underground movement carried out its mission. The author had no official rank. The German invasion found him stranded in France and, after unsuccessful attempts to join the allied forces in Africa, he searched for the "resistance", found it, was admitted into the movement and worked as one of its ordinary members. His goal was his duty towards his country and, as he wished to remain free in order to be able to go there where he would be most useful, he always refused to be bound to any particular group.

As the events described are still recent, the real names of persons and places concerned are not given. Approximately, the theatre of operations may be thus limited: the region of the central mountain chain which extends from the Rhône Valley to the fertile plains south of Paris. This part of France is inhabited principally by a people of industrious, weather-beaten and kind peasants, much akin to our "Canny Scot" by their exact knowledge of the value of money, who have given to their country such heroes as Vercingetorix.

Few European countries provided so many material advantages as France for the organisation of a secret army. Obligatory military training makes every adult Frenchman a soldier. The underground movement thus found an army all trained and ready for action. Younger men who had not yet accomplished their military training but had learned to look upon its coming as a necessity, found soldiering a natural event in their lives.

The nature itself of this widespread country which can boast of comprising all the European climates was ideal for guerrilla warfare. Whole armies can be concealed on the thickly pine-wooded slopes of Alsace, on the rocky coasts or in the vast and lovely agricultural stretches of Brittany. The central chain, the Alps and the Pyrenees lend themselves naturally to ambushes. Their very position would give to armies occupying these strongholds every advantage in case of attack and the possibility of rendering useless or even impossible any great scale operations on the part of the enemy army.

The very French temperament, fiery, imaginative, idealistic, which, at the end of the eighteenth and the beginning of the nineteenth century, gave to a starving and ragged army of volunteers the strength and courage to defend successfully its frontiers against coalesced invaders while the interior of the country was swamped in post-revolutionary misery and disorder, was a fertile ground for the seed of General de Gaulle's call to patriotism, generosity and sacrifice.

May this "récit" revive the souvenir[1] of the heroes of a nameless and homeless army and an everlasting tribute of thanks to the generous peasants to whom more than one "maquisard" owes his life.

---

[1] *memory*

The canteen seemed to reel. The multicoloured uniforms of my comrades in arms of the French Colonial Army became a brilliant whirlpool about my head. Unsteadily I made my way to one of the little canteen tables still holding my unemptied glass of wine. All around me the others had taken up their conversation after the amazed silence which had followed the news given by the wireless only a few seconds ago. The majority of the soldiers taken from nearly all the French Colonial Regiment and who found themselves here in the Colonial Dépôt at Marseilles were there pending departure for North Africa. The majority had been on leave, a few had newly joined-up and all seemed highly pleased with the news they had just learned. I looked at them and realised that I too should be happy. The allies have landed in North Africa and seemed to be consolidating their position. I was a British subject, although in the Foreign Legion as the Swiss Jean Daubry. As such I should have been happier than anyone else, I had a right to be happier. My own countrymen had scored a definite advantage. Soon the draught-like movement of the British forces in Libya and Tripolitania would cease. The Germans and Italians would be definitely chased out of Africa and, I knew it in my heart, France's turn would come soon after. Yes, I should be happy and I knew it but my gladness was tinged with regret. I had done so much to arrive where I was. I had dreamed of reaching Africa, joining the British troops over there and doing my duty in this war. I did not know how I could have managed it but it was the end I had in view in joining the Legion. My reason was happy but my heart was not. I had come through so much to be where I now was. All my efforts to reach Africa had been in vain.

In 1939 I was a student in Lyon, the end of my studies was not far off but when in August of 1939 in Brittany, where I was teaching in a small private school, I learned that war was at hand I immediately went to Paris to interview the British chief consul. He advised me to continue with my studies, took my name and address in Lyon and promised to inform me if I was needed. He persuaded me of the utter foolishness of returning home precipitately and leaving my studies so near the end. When war was declared the consul in Lyon was unable to be of any help.

Then came the terrible 10th May, 1940. The Germans had invaded Holland and Luxemburg. News had been quite good, too good even because really too laconic "our men are holding their positions", "we have taken so many prisoners". In spite of this optimism I often asked myself why the skies were so free of German bombers? Where were the allied planes? But the truth was not far away. A trickle of cars which soon became a regular stream began to people the roads. At first only civilian vehicles were to be seen but soon army cars carrying officers and bearing all the traces of a hasty flight flew along towards the south. And then came the most pitiful sight of all: civilians on foot, thousands of them, carrying bundles, pushing wheelbarrows and trying to console weeping children. Like a film the past two years ran before my mind's eye. All the sentiments inspired by the German invasion and occupation flowed back into my mind. A profound pity for that endless stream of refugees, harassed and haggard, who knew only one refrain which put an end to all persuasion to rest: "farther south, farther south; the Germans are coming". The stories they told and the rumours which accompanied them were heart-breaking: everywhere disorder: fifth columnists in every town and village. The Germans did not need petrol for their tanks; a few pastilles in a pail of water and everything was in order. There was devastation everywhere. The situation was bad and everyone knew it but I had still hoped against hope that something would happen. The French broadcasting service could only play the Marseillaise and say that our troops were holding their positions. Radio Stuttgart spoke with abundant details of the relentless advance of the German troops but everyone was inclined to disbelieve it. In spite of all, I did not lose hope. I was in no way afraid but could not bear to think that I would have to stay there helpless or be taken prisoner without having had a chance to fire a shot while many of my countrymen had died in trying to stop the invasion. And then came the shock. Early one afternoon the German tanks clattered into the town. All the previous day I had heard the fighting a few miles away. I had asked my superior for the permission and the money to leave for Bordeaux (I would still have had time) but this had been coldly refused. It was useless to try to take to the road because I would only have swelled the unending stream which was already obstructing them; No way of having any help from the British Consulate because this consul had left and the only one to be found was his French secretary who told me that I might get a boat at Bordeaux but never thought of offering me any means of arriving there. All she could do was take my name and details concerning those who were to be warned in case of accident. So there I was. My spirits were far from high and sight of those tanks with the large Nazi swastika unfolded over their front made me feel sick. Never before had I realised how much I hated the Germans. I was not worried about being made prisoner, in fact I did not care what happened to me, it was what was going to happen next that worried me. France could not hold on much longer, and did not because very soon afterwards came the news of the armistice, but what annoyed me more than anything else was the rumour that Britain had also given in. What a mental torture until I had confirmation of the contrary. I felt as though a weight had been taken off my shoulders when I was sure that Britain was still holding out. I might yet be able to do something and this became the goal of my thoughts and efforts. The Free-French broadcasts became so to speak my daily bread. General de Gaulle's first calls to the French people in favour of the "Résistance" were a refreshing balm to my heart and mind because the atmosphere of the country was anything but pro-British. As time went on after the armistice the anti-British sentiment, although happily not universal, became very prevalent in the country. Fostered by the occupants, by state broadcasts, by many of the newspapers, the word went around that Britain had abandoned France. She had been unprepared for war, and had sent only a very small expeditionary force which she had hastened to withdraw at Dunkirk. Her air-force had been ridiculously small, so small, in fact, that it had been non-existent. Food was becoming very scarce and again the fault was Britain's. The British Navy was stopping all shipping coming from North Africa and the French colonies. This unjust propaganda found a great echo among the generality of the French people because the situation was really terrible. The country had 2,000,000 men behind German barbed wire and was suffering from a moral and nervous breakdown. It was to this morally sick people that General de Gaulle made his appeal. Knowing the people and having an idea of the capacity of their generosity and courage, I was sure that many would answer to it but it would be a difficult task. This country was in a pitiful state both morally and physically.

As time went on the situation become worse. Food became more and more scarce. The absence of their prisoners was a terrible drawback for the economy of the country. The occupying army was a heavy financial burden and its presence an everyday humiliation. Marshall Petain, chief of the then French state, as it was called, founded a legion for the ex-servicemen of both wars which had for its goal the county's revival. The majority had responded to his call and almost every buttonhole was owned with the insignia of the ancient French double-sided battle-axe. Exteriorly events gave little hope and, as everyone understood, the country could only depend on help from the outside. By herself France could really do nothing efficacious to better her situation. The Russians had made a pact with the Germans. Great Britain was being bombed day and night (the B.B.C. spoke of the number of German planes brought down but the Germans gave their own figures and no one had any means of controlling the veracity of either. Many disbelieved the Germans statements but others were just as sceptical about the British declarations). The Balkans were in German hands, Turkey's attitude uncertain. There were the backward and forward movements in Africa. In the face of all this, many were of the opinion that Britain should give in. She was all alone and her stubbornness was responsible both for the absence of the French prisoners (if the war was over they would be liberated) and the precarious alimentary and economic situation of the country (if war ended they could sign a definite peace with Germany. The strain of the upkeep of the occupying army would cease and trade could be taken up again). I suffered terribly from this selfish point of view. I saw the moral beauty of my country's courage and confidence and it gave me a new life and strength to fight against such a depressing atmosphere. The caustic remarks of those around me only roused my determination to contact the movement pioneered by General de Gaulle; but where was I to find it? Casual enquiries, unhappily limited and hampered by my particular situation, gave no positive result. As time went on the political situation became worse. Laval forced himself into the government and the ex-servicemen's legion from a country-rebuilding movement became a definitely political organisation destined to prove and realise Franco-German collaboration. The situation became more and more serious for anyone who was searching for the Résistance movement because one did not know every person's ideas and it was exceedingly dangerous to speak to anyone. Communists were pointed out as public enemy number one and it was quite simple. At that time, to have people imprisoned as such. In fact anyone who criticised the government's attitude was immediately looked upon as a communist and treated as such. In a few words, the government was giving in little by little to the Germans and we had the impression that it was not Frenchmen but the occupiers who were governing the country. I saw that the situation was void of security. My British identity put me in immediate danger. Any day I might be taken and led away prisoner. What an outlook! To be behind barbed wire while my countrymen were fighting against such huge odds! One solution was open to me. My superiors had a house at Marseilles and Marseilles was near to Africa where my countrymen were fighting. However, the difficulties were numberless. How could I persuade my superiors to send me there and even then how could I stay there as all foreigners had to obtain a special permission to leave their established address and the coastline counties were "out of bounds and forbidden territory for any British subject"?

And, even if I arrived there, how would I cross to French North Africa and from there to the British troops? Trusting in my lucky star I saw one of my friends, a doctor, who persuaded my superiors that my health was really bad and that the Mediterranean climate was the only hope for me. This initial success encouraged me and I undertook the formalities necessary to obtain the permission for my change of address. I was not given much hope but as the government, in order to try and secure their help, was favourable to everything that seemed clerical, I received my papers after about a month's writing.

When I arrived in Marseilles it seemed to me that across the blue waters of the "Vieux Port" I could see Africa. I had no money at all and there seemed only one solution: stow away in a boat and work my passage but experience taught me to be careful. Marseilles was a nest of traitors and profiteers. One day, as I was walking in the shade in the "Allées de Luyan", just off the famous "Canebière", I was accosted by a middle-aged man dressed in working clothes and who wore, rather too ostensibly in his buttonhole a rather too highly coloured sickle and hammer. After the usual greetings and commonplace remarks on the weather he began to criticise the then French government and to vaunt the communists and their untiring work for their country. He spoke of underground movements in general and, in a confidential manner, of a special movement he knew very well and asked me what I thought about them. Until then I had spoken politely but on his last confidences I simply rose and, after looking at him and saying something more or less polite, walked off. At this time there were also so-called secret organisations who, for a certain fee, promised to bring people over the Pyrenees into Spain or in small boats out to liners or even British boats who were to bring them to Africa or even to Great Britain. The would-be clients were sworn to secrecy in secret meeting-places (which were never the same) but the same fates usually awaited them. When they arrived at the rendezvous they either met members of the Gestapo or Italian police or else they found nobody and lost all the money they had already paid (half had to be paid in advance). I realised that I was in a blind alley. I had not come to Marseilles to be caught in a trap but to use it as a springboard to reach Africa. It was thus very dangerous to try any irregular channel because of the wholesale traffic of those who profited from desperate situations to enrichen themselves either by selling unfortunate people for German gold or by swindling them in the meanest ways. I even came to suspect almost everyone. After reflection there was only one way open to me and that was an official way. Marseilles' streets were highly coloured by the elegant uniforms of the French Colonial Armistice Army. The sight of the white képis of the Foreign Legion gave me an idea and, as soon as it was possible I put it into execution. After having informed myself of the whereabouts of the recruiting office I went there in April 1942 but was refused at the medical visit because of my teeth. In spite of my discouraged remark that a soldier had other arms than these, I was sent away. Then began a hide and seek game with my superiors to remedy the fault. After some discussions I found a friendly dentist who promised to look after me for a moderate sum. As the work was cheap I received my superior's consent without their knowing the reason for my sudden desire. When at last all was ready I slipped away and on the 26th October, 1942, I became lègionnaire Jean Daubry, born in Geneva, Rue du Lac on the 25th April, 1916 (I had taken as my address Rue du Lac because I had learned that there was no Rue de la Gare in the town. Life changed for me but I liked the gruff, straightforwardness of the officers and the simple and artless friendship of the men. For my first night in barracks I had neither sheets nor pillow but a friendly old lègionnaire gave me his best greatcoat to put under my head for the night. Next day a private interview by the captain and lieutenant who was in the 2° Bureau. There I was obliged to tell me real identity which was noted in a special register as also was the name of those to be notified in the case of mortal accident. My passport was taken from me. The captain was quite surprised at finding a British subject and, in his abrupt way asked me what I would do if I was asked to fight against my former countrymen. I immediately replied that I would do my duty but the captain, who was as unassuming as myself, asked what my duty would be. I simply replied that I would see if such circumstances offered themselves. From that day onwards I experienced the hard Legion discipline but was quite happy because of the thought that I would soon be in Africa. The mentality was good and the majority, with the exception of a few who had come back from leave and who had fought in Syria against the Allies, were definitely pro-British. I realised that I was not the only one to have the idea of deserting to join the British troops and it encouraged me.

Then came the so good and yet so dreadful news, positively good but psychologically dreadful. Everything would have to be begun all over again! I was not the possible difficulties which annoyed me but, after having given up everything to reach my goal, I was in danger of being brought to a complete standstill and put in the impossibility of ever doing anything for my country. What was going to happen now? If only we could try and put up an armed resistance now that Africa had given the example. It was with rather mixed thoughts that I made my way to our depot. I had not long to wait.

The bugle rang out. Assembly! Men ran out at the double and the company formed up rapidly in the square. After the ritual "Attention! Stand easy!" the captain came out of his office at the top of the square and, in the usual abrupt but friendly way which had won him the hearts of the men, he explained the situation. "As you all know by now the Allies have landed in North Africa. Certain officers and men of the French Colonial Army have joined them. The Germans have erased the demarcation line and have occupied militarily the whole country. They are even now in the town. You are all confined to barracks and must await orders. I do not know what we will have to do but in any case neither the officers nor the N.C.O.s will leave you. Be confident. I shall do my very best for all. Long live the Légion! Dismiss!" Nobody knew what to think but there was a general feeling of insecurity. During the following days the wireless and an occasional newspaper gave further details: the Allies were advancing in Africa but the German soldiers occupied all the important centres as well as the strategic points in France. One day all the soldiers of the depot had quite a surprise. In the morning we heard very heavy artillery fire and, in our part of the camp which overlooked the sea we crowded along the barbed-wire to try to discover what was happening. It was heavy coastal defence manoeuvres but one wag sent the word around that the Allies were trying to land on the coast. It was really astonishing to see how these men who knew within themselves how highly improbable was such an event hoped against hope that it was true. In our situation I understood how much one hopes for anything, even the most absurd.

The Germans were there in the town as they were in every important centre. No one had any identity papers. Even the eight who were coming back from leave had only their military papers. All the new recruits' papers were in the lieutenant's office. If they had had their identity cards many of the soldiers could perhaps have deserted because they were French but a good number had joined the Legion to escape from one thing or another so they were not keen on facing civil life. Others were, like myself, in a more dangerous position because they were foreigners and certain ones could not even speak French. These especially were in a dangerous position because they were deserters from the German army – one a pure-blooded German, one Yugoslavian and one from Alsace-Lorraine where conscription had been imposed. We were there helpless with no idea of what was going to happen to us. If the government chose to give us up to the enemy to swell the already huge army of prisoners and voluntary or involuntary industrial workers sought daily by the Germans, it would be an ignominious end to our adventure. I decided to make a bid for freedom but would not go away without my passport which, in spite of the danger it would put me in, appeared to me more precious than ever before. The captain's secretary, who knew my real identity (he was, I think, the only one outside of the chief officer's) had become very friendly with me. Although of a lonely nature I encouraged his friendship, seeing in it a way of recovering my identity papers. He had made no secret to me of his pro-British sentiments and, after the North African landing and its results for us, spoke to me quite often of desertion to avoid being taken by the enemy. The day after this great event I told him of my intention of going away and asked him to help me to get my passport. He accepted most willingly and the next day I had the precious booklet in my possession once again. We began to make plans but were not allowed to put them into execution. From the day of the Allied landing we were ordered to stand-to for action and were never allowed to undress at night. Sentries were doubled all over the depot and we were very frequently assembled in the square. Something was brewing but we did not know what. Two or three days later we were called about midnight and, as our packs had been by order kept ready, we were soon formed up in the square. The captain spoke to us, asking us to believe him and obey his orders scrupulously. We were leaving the barracks and had to follow our officers in silence. Through the obscurity of the complete blackout we went noiselessly across the sleeping town. After about an hour's march we arrived at a big barracks and were billeted, 150 strong, in a long loft. Here I realised how much the regular army looked upon the Legion as pariahs. During our short stay in this very modern and well-equipped barracks we were obliged to sleep on straw mattresses without sheets in this long but very low loft and had to take our food outside sitting on the ground in the square. Happily we had no bad weather. Here my friend and I had no chance to plan desertion. Our time was very well taken up by exercises of all sorts and, five or six days after our arrival, we had another nightly summons and were marched, this time, to the station where a train of most uncomfortable cattle trucks awaited us. After an all-night journey which lasted until about mid-day the next day we arrived in a small but quite important town near the end of the central chain of mountains. Here our quarters were a little more comfortable and we were better treated. We shared the barracks with an Indochinese regiment with which we had little or no contact. Had we been allowed to associate with them there would certainly have been trouble because the Légionnaires are born fighters. They seem to have this instinct in the blood. For the first two days we were confined to barracks as usual but for the remainder of the time we were allowed into town in small numbers. Here three of our men deserted but were brought back two days afterwards. They had no ration books and because of the presence of enemy troops everywhere nobody would help them for fear of reprisals. In spite of this and the severity with which we were guarded, my companion and I decided to attempt a getaway when all of a sudden we were again given orders pack and marched off to the station where a train waited to carry us once more to an unknown destination. Here a mistake was made.

We were issued with food for a journey which lasted exactly twenty-seven hours. When we arrived at our new barracks we were all well-nigh exhausted. Our new quarters were very good and very comfortable, too good in fact and too comfortable to last long. One fine morning at about eleven o'clock (it was a Thursday and a week after our arrival) the barracks was completely surrounded by an enemy column and in a few minutes four armoured cars lined up in the square held us at attention. We were quickly ordered to offer no resistance but, to say the truth, we had not the least chance of so because of the unexpectedness and suddenness of the attack. We were really and truly prisoners this time. Our quarters and persons were thoroughly searched. Happily for myself I had hidden my identity papers in quite an ordinary place but the German officer did not think of it or did not want to look there. Fearing that the disappearance of my passport would be noticed I had torn out the empty visa pages and, after softening the covers, had managed to put it in my boot between the insole and the sole. I breathed quite a sigh of relief when the search was ended. These formalities over, the officer in command of the enemy unit reassembled us and in perfect French told us that we were his prisoners pending the French government's decision as to what they were going to do with the armistice army. He painted the German violation of the treaty as an act rendered necessary by the "treachery" of the North African troops who had rallied to the Allied standard during and after the landing. No harm would befall us if we obeyed orders. From then until we were demobilised three days afterwards we were quite well treated but were given very little liberty. On the evening of the second day of "captivity" we were given twenty-four hours to leave the barracks. All of us were to leave our uniforms and equipment behind and be dressed only in civilian clothes. Those not conforming to these orders would be made regular prisoners. It was a hectic twenty-four hours. The N.C.O.'s worked all night making out our demobilisation papers. When my turn came I went to my own sergeant who was of German origin and who had been obliged to leave his country for personal but very important reasons. I explained to him that I could return to civilian life neither with my false Swiss identity (if ever I had to go to see a Swiss consul or if the French wished to repatriate me my case would be hopeless) nor with my real British identity – could he do anything for me? His answer was a hearty handshake and a question as to what name, nationality and birthplace I wished to have in the important and official papers. I chose my name, kept my own date of birth and took Lyon as my birthplace because it was the town I knew best. Later I was more than thankful for this precious paper which took me out of many a tight corner. Thanks to it I was able to have a regular identity card, ration books and, what was more precious to me than anything else, I could go anywhere I pleased in the country without restraint. This was exceedingly important for me because on leaving the Legion I had, so to speak, nowhere to go and needed to be absolutely free of movement.

However, Saturday morning came, the day on which we had to evacuate the barracks. Immediately after dinner we were assembled in the square and issued with a civilian suit and two days' rations. After changing, our demobilisation papers were given to us and we were marched to the station in groups of fifteen. It was not a very simple matter to become accustomed to a new name. When mine was called the first time I did not recognise it and the N.C.O. hearing no reply called it out again very loudly. Realising that the German officers were looking on and not wishing to cause any suspicion I stepped out of the ranks reeling a little as if I had celebrated too well our liberation. Many smiled but I only felt really safe when our small section was completed and we were on our way to the station singing as the "légionnaires" do in every circumstance. There we were met by a lady from the Red Cross and given a little tobacco and some cigarette papers. What a pleasure to smoke a real cigarette. The good smokes had been very few and far between during the last month.

I sat down on a bench to think my situation over. I had known that we were being sent back to civil life, I had wondered where I could go and my choice had fallen upon a hospital of the congregation to which I belonged and which was about eighty to ninety miles from my last barracks. Would I be accepted there as a nurse? The situation was delicate and very serious for me. I felt quite sure that the hospital director would not send me away but then one never knows. And there is always a certain uneasiness when one contemplates the unknown. Here I was with nothing but the clothes I was wearing. In my small army satchel were two days' rations. I had just about enough money to enable me to live parsimoniously for two days. Happily my army papers dispensed me from paying my railway fare. I had left everything, burned my boats, so to speak, and here I was farther from Africa and the Allied army than ever. However, as the Arabs say: "Nuktoub", it is written and must be so. I looked upon the situation quite philosophically, determined to make the best of it. My ideas had not changed and, given a chance, I might be able to do something. Why did the enemy let us go? Etc. Soon the train arrived, an express, and, accompanied by another ex-légionnaire, I climbed into it. Ten minutes later we arrived in the station where I was to change. The local train was waiting. I climbed into a carriage where I saw another young man who, by his dress, was certainly a demobilised soldier like myself. The train was not due to leave until half an hour later but we were just as well in it as on the platform. We began to talk and, over a snack taken from our rations, were soon good friends. My companion, who had been billeted in the town, told me that one of his friends had been killed by the Germans when they came to take the barracks and its occupants. He was on sentry duty. As the intruders did not reply to his challenge he had raised his rifle to fire. On this movement they had shot him dead and at the same time their leading tank had burst the main gate open. It was very quickly done. We were chatting in a very friendly way when we noticed German soldiers gathering around the train. The explanation was not late in coming. The stationmaster informed us that the whole carriage was reserved for the "Wermacht". We gathered up our few belongings and were preparing to look for another carriage when a German officer put in his head and told us not to hurry. "The war is now over for you," said he with a smile. "Yes, but not for you," replied my companion. The officer's smile faded but I could not help smiling myself. After finding another compartment we began our monotonous climb. What a journey! My friend had only about twenty kilométres to do but I had almost four times as much. It took the train about four hours to do approximately eighty kilométres. I left at 6.00 p.m. and arrived at my destination at 9.45 p.m. The station scarcely deserved the name; it was only a small halt and owed its existence to the presence of the hospital. I had heard that the latter was isolated and very far from everything but did not dare believe it as lonely as I was to learn the next day. It was pitch black when I arrived – no lights at all. The stationmaster informed me that the hospital offices were closed but showed me the way to a small hotel (the only one within a radius of five miles). After a perilous mile's walk along the river bank only a few yards wide, which ended on one side in a sheer wall of rock and on the other in a frozen river, I arrived at the "hôtel", in reality a small café, the hospital's electrical power station, which boasted of two rooms for guests. I think I was never as cold in all my life and was pleased to find a clean and comfortable bed in which I found after an hour or so a certain amount of warmth. I had been asked no questions and that was the most important thing. Early next morning I was received by the hospital director who recognised me and, understanding my situation, made no difficulty in accepting me. After a good meal I was given a room and brought to the pavilion where I was hereafter to work. My patients were the lowest class of M.O.s but their quarters were the farthest away from the hospital entrance and their repulsive condition did not encourage visitors, which fact was a decided advantage for me. It was agreed that I should be known there even by the office staff by my borrowed name. Thanks to my army papers I soon had a regular identity card and ration books. In a word, everything had worked out perfectly well. From a poorly lad and friendless wanderer I had now become a member of the staff of a recognised mental hospital. My life and comfort were assured. My perfect knowledge of the language and regular papers put me above suspicion. The situation of the hospital, five miles from the nearest village and twenty from the first important town hid me from too inquisitive enquiries.

But I had joined the Foreign Legion with the intention to join the Allied forces. My plans had been frustrated but my ideas were unchanged. The only way of doing anything useful now was to contact the "résistance" and offer my services. This I set out to do. Being a stranger in the country I had to be very cautious as I kept my ears and eyes open. I soon found that the region was an "underground" centre. Often I heard tell of one thing or another but after trying to follow the traces I never had any success. The small underground groups were then better formed than ever they were later and absolutely hermetic. Passwords were very secret, just as hidden as certain activities. Often wives ignored the activity of their husbands and parents knew nothing of their sons' underground work. One had to be known and well recommended to enter into contact with any group. My efforts were rendered in vain by a fact that, until then, had escaped me. When one has had a good education and has lived in a certain sphere for a few years one's manner and speech carry a certain mark. I spoke French perfectly but too perfectly for a simple nurse in a mental hospital. I was much too polite and well-spoken for my situation and in this age of spies and general danger for anyone who had not the same ideas as the government I must have seemed suspicious. I realised this too late but the harm had been done. The situation was too delicate; I could not tell all these I suspected of underground activity my real nationality nor, above all, could I show them my authentic papers because if I happened to have made a mistake…? The Germans gave very important rewards for the capture of underground agents and would certainly have enlarged upon them for the capture of a British subject about whom it could have been simple to make up a story. The enemy usually asked few questions in these cases. All my efforts to realise my ambition seemed of no avail. I had been in my new situation over six months and found nothing. I was beginning to despair but "the darkest hour comes just before the dawn".

One day while we were at lunch the director, contrary to his habits, came to our dining hall and called me. His mysterious and unusual manner made me wonder if I had done anything wrong or if my secret had transpired in any way. I was prepared to defend my life but I wished to avoid any annoyance for the hospital. We crossed the hall and, entering into a private room where he bade me sit down, my employer told me the story which was to change my life and give me the so long hoped for chance. A friend, dentist in the region, had a British airman in his home. He needed an interpreter and had asked the director if any of the members of his community knew sufficient English to help. Several of them did but he did not wish them to go as he was responsible for them and the safety of the hospital. However, as he was a great patriot, he wished to help and so had decided to speak to me about it. After warning me of all the dangers of the mission and insisting on the perfect secrecy of the whole business, he made me understand that I was in no way obliged to respond to his call. Whether I wished to help or not I was left free for the afternoon. I was only too pleased and immediately after lunch I made my way to the address indicated.

The dentist was delighted when he learned the reason for my visit. I gave no details. I had simply heard of the airman's presence and had come to act as an interpreter. During his visits to the hospital the dentist had already seen me but he did not know my real identity. The airman in question was a young Canadian pilot who had been obliged to bale out over the north of France. His story was quite extraordinary but he had an accent of sincerity which put his narrative beyond all doubt. After the shooting down of his plane he had been offered shelter by some peasants who had given him civilian clothes. As they had been unable to put him in contact with any organisation he had made up his mind to try to reach the Spanish frontier. Although he knew no French he had been extremely lucky. Thanks to maps he had with him and a small compass hidden in a tunic button he had succeeded in making his way south and had accomplished about half his journey on arriving in our region. His manner of proceeding had been to stop before reaching the important stations where papers were invariably controlled, take to the country, avoid the important agglomerations and take the train farther on. So long as his food reserve and money had lasted he had been able to continue but, on arriving in the town where I met him, he had been exhausted and almost penniless. Trusting to his lucky star he had made himself known as well as possible to the proprietor of a small hôtel who, thinking that the dentist knew sufficient English, had passed him on to him. When I met him he had been there three days. He had been staying in the house all the time, only going out for a few minutes after nightfall to have a little fresh air. As one can well understand he was far from comfortable. His only means of proving his identity were: his identity disc, the insignia of his regiment which he had kept, his compass which was a disguised RAF button, his maps on silk handkerchiefs and a small container of concentrated rations. These may, and did, seem small proofs but, when questioned and more questioned he had an unmistakable accent of sincerity. He did not wish to be a burden to anyone. His goal remained the same; the Spanish frontier. There were, however, several difficulties besides the financial problem which was the least of all: we had to procure a false identity card on which, because of his ignorance of the language, he would need to be declared deaf and dumb. As the enemy had declared all the Atlantic and channel shores as well as the land around the Franco-Spanish border special territory, special papers were needed for non-habitual residents there and control was very severe. Even if he did succeed in gaining the border he would need someone to bring him across in a quiet place otherwise he risked being sent back or placed in a concentration camp. In any case he would need someone to accompany him. The problem was considerable and complicated but was interesting and certainly worth a trial. I promised to do all I could and left him with a definite plan in mind.

At that time the Germans were taking everything they could from the country and, among other things, the rails from the railroad tracks which were not indispensable. This operation was being carried out on the line which ran past the hospital. Two young railway engineers were supervising the conversion of the double track into a single one and had taken over, in the interim, the small station. One of them was from the south of France and the other a native of the region. As they were quite far from their respective homes they took their meals with us and, during the conversations, I had learned that the former had a sister who lived almost on the Spanish frontier. While speaking to John, the airman, I thought of this fact and decided to ask Bertrand if he would accept to help him. On the first occasion I put the question to him explaining the whole situation. His reply baffled me at the beginning but I realised later that he was trying to see if I was a member of the underground. "The birds are flying low" said he looking at me very closely but, as I did not reply, he came quickly back to the subject and promised, a little vaguely, that he would see what could be done. His curious reply preyed on my mind and, little by little, I became more and more certain that he was in the movement. Late that evening when my work was finished I went down to the station and, finding him in company with Louis, his comrade, asked if I could see him alone. He seemed to guess the reason for my coming and told me to speak out in front of Louis. I "put all my cards on the table" showing my passport to prove my sincerity. How pleased they were! In turn they told me that they had both belonged to the "résistance" and would do what they could for John. Louis asked to see him and we planned the meeting for the next evening. I telephoned to the dentist fixing a rendezvous. Accordingly, late in the afternoon, we met in the dentist's waiting room and were introduced into the house where, for Louis's peace of mind, I cross-questioned John. When he was satisfied he left and returned a little more than an hour later with the news that John was to be ready to leave with us near midnight for an unknown destination where he would be put into safe hands. I telephoned to the director of the hospital telling him I was spending a night with friends and would report for duty next morning and awaited events. True to his word Louis arrived near 11.30 p.m. on his bicycle. The dentist's wife lent me her cycle and we found another for John. Of the three I was the only one to have a lamp but we did not attach any importance to this fact because the town was very small and we did not expect any trouble. However we were really out of luck. We had scarcely left the town when we were met by a patrol of four gendarmes. Louis was in the lead with John and I following. We were ordered to stop and dismount. The leader of the patrol, a sergeant, asked to see identity cards. I began to feel uneasy. We were definitely unlucky because Louis had forgotten his card. Seeing him searching in his pockets I hastily tendered mine, hoping thus to distract their attention from him and above all from John. It was quite a tight corner because although some of the gendarmes were very favourable to the "underground" others were fanatical collaborationists. While the patrol sergeant was examining my card another gendarme was looking over his shoulder and, in the light of the pocket lamp, his face seemed familiar. When he had seen my name and my photo he immediately turned towards me with a smile and asked me how everybody at the hospital was. I then recognised him as one of the gendarmes who came frequently to the hospital for one reason or another and who had dined beside me more than once. On seeing this the sergeant's manner softened. He asked me what we were doing on the road with no lights at this time of night. I replied that I felt a needed a little relaxation after being closed in for so long with the patients and that we were going to a dance in a village a few miles away. He smiled and, after admonishing us to be more careful in future, bade us goodnight. We breathed a sigh of relief when they disappeared from view.

In a few minutes we arrived at our destination, a small cluster of houses. We stopped at the last one and after awaiting Louis, who entered first, were soon in the presence of one of the finest "résistance" members I have known. He was small, very strong and, until known, very gruff. Immediately he got down to business. I told how I had met John and, acting as interpreter, made him tell his own story. To convince him of our veracity I put all John's insignia on the table and, beside them my passport. His reply was sudden and unexpected. Besides the papers, etc, he put a revolver: "Tell him that if has told a lie he will never leave this house alive. He will stay here for a few days until I can arrange for his departure for England but during this time he will only be allowed out at night accompanied by me and my colt." I translated for John and insisted upon the necessity of complete submission to orders. He replied "Yeah" and immediately our new friend jumped to his feet: "But he is a German." "Why?" I replied. "Did he not say Ja?" I smiled and explained that "Yeah", which sounded so much like the German was his Canadian and American "yes". He was not quite convinced but after hearing us speak together for a certain time he seemed more at ease. Once he was one of us he showed us a little of his real self; a well of kindness. Even the best he had in his home was not good enough to celebrate, as he colourfully put it, "the presence under his roof of His Majesty's subjects". John continued to live in his home until D.14 (our friend's "résistance" number) got in contact with his chiefs who were to arrange for his repatriation. He was definitely unlucky. The landing ground where British planes came to deliver and take errands or persons had been discovered and rendered useless by the enemy. John was then transferred to a château where the proprietor, a lady, spoke English. Then he was taken by an agent who brought him to the Spanish frontier only to learn that the six local gendarmes who did the "passing" had been betrayed and arrested prior to facing a firing squad. This reprisal had cooled the local "résistants"' ardour and as nobody would accept the mission our airman was brought back. Another unsuccessful effort was made to send him back to England. An agent brought him to Brittany where a fisherman tried to cross to England. Halfway across the sea the little boat sprang a leak and they had to turn back baling out the water and happy to regain the French coast. John then took to the "maquis" and fought there against the Germans until he could join the advancing Allied forces and regain his unit. His adventures would make quite an interesting book. (Letter can be produced to prove this story.)

From this time onwards I had the joy of making myself actively useful as a liaison agent. D.14 was a very active member of the "iron résistance" (railway) group. If the Germans had only known the plans of factories, roads, bridges, movements of troops with details of regiments etc. and munitions which were carried by the very trains they were using they would have been more careful. Very often when D.14 was called elsewhere either by his own work or other activity I received at the small hospital halt, on a special sign, papers which were of great importance. Our signs were simple: a particular attitude, a sign with a handkerchief, a special way of smoking or holding a cigarette and the engine driver, stoker or guard would reply in the agreed way and slip deftly into the palm of your hand a well-folded cigarette paper or two which often contained the RAF's object on its next bombing mission. My day's work over in the hospital, I set out after nightfall to walk almost five miles along the railroad to deliver my precious message to D.14 or his wife. Their house was a district "letter box". Here I had the pleasure of meeting a few of the more important members of the movement. All had the same characteristics: simplicity, courage and devotedness to the cause. I never knew any of their names and they never knew mine. The men and women had numbers and, while the former had boys' and animals' names, the latter were all called after birds. Many of them I only knew for a short time because their life was one of permanent danger but one event caused the loss of the lives of four of them and put D.14 in great peril. One of our agents, whom I knew very well and who was called "Engine Driver" turned traitor without our knowing it.

We received the news in a strange but very dangerous way. One morning I received from the stationmaster of our little halt a closed envelope without stamp which had come, said he, by train. On opening it I read: "Two parcels received yesterday evening. Could you come and help unpack them?" I was quite puzzled and the afternoon seemed very long. My duty ended I took to the railroad and made my way to D.14's home as quickly as possible. I found him in his garden behind the house. He seemed quite worried. "Late last night two British airmen were brought here. They are upstairs. They have come to me through regular channels but I don't know why I do not feel comfortable about them. Of course I felt the same about John and he was genuine. I will feel more at ease when you will have questioned them." We went upstairs. The newcomers were certainly British-looking. They had the same means of identification as John had given us and spoke perfect English. Two facts, however, surprised me: they did not seem too pleased to see a fellow-countryman (I remember how overjoyed John was) and their demeanour was very rigid. The story seemed plausible enough but their rigidity and lack of humour struck me. They did not seem at all willing to undertake a free and easy conversation as two men deprived of speaking with any others except themselves should naturally have been delighted to be. They contented themselves with questions and answers. The making of conversation was left to me. Before leaving in the early hours of the morning I shared my impressions with my friend. Although he could only follow the details of the conversation through my interpretation he had the same impression as myself. Like myself he had compared their attitude and reactions to those of John and the comparison was decidedly unfavourable. He decided to keep a watchful eye on his guests while conducting a serious enquiry. Late in the afternoon I was called to the office to answer a telephone call.

The dentist was inviting me to tea and would not accept a refusal. I understood that something was wrong and asked to have the evening off. The director, who had an idea that I was working with the "underground" granted the permission without hesitation. On my way to the station I met the dentist. He had telephoned from a small café on the main road and, on receiving my reply, had continued on his motorcycle to the hospital. D.14 was awaiting me. He did not know why but it seemed important. In a few minutes we had arrived. I left the dentist in the town and, following a country path was soon at my destination. After the usual conversation D.14

bade me tell the airmen that we were taking them to a new hiding place and that they were to prepare their small kit. While they were thus occupied and on the pretext that we were going to see if the road was clear he explained the situation: four of our friends had been arrested simultaneously and the German and French special police seemed to have, according to their movements, precise information regarding the regional "underground". Some of our prominent members had been very lucky to be warned in time and had had to leave precipitously. He suspected our guests of being part of this movement and had decided to steer clear. He showed me his revolver and I verified mine. "They might be armed," said he, "so be on the qui vive."

When all was ready we set out, telling our protégés to be very cautious. D.14 led us from the main road to a quite narrow path through a thick wood. Only two could walk abreast so he bade them to walk together in front so that they could converse a little. When we were a certain distance from the road D.14 whipped out his revolver and curtly, from behind, ordered them to stop and raise their hands. Their reaction betrayed them. They understood French well enough. Both turned quickly, one with a revolver in his hand, a German Maüser, while the other was reaching for his. We both fired simultaneously. I killed the one who was ready to shoot and who was on my side while the other fell with a bullet in the stomach. Before he died the latter told us, with a sneer on his face, that our organisation's activity was at an end. From his description of the traitor we understood that we had been sold by our friend "Engine Driver". Later this man was captured, tried and shot. His lust for money had cost more than fifty lives among which were many valuable agents. We buried these two Gestapo members in a small but deep stagnant pool. But the whereabouts of our letterbox was now known. A very short time afterwards D.14 escaped by jumping from an attic window into his garden while the enemy police were climbing the staircase. With the help of false papers and the connivance of his employers he reached Paris where he continued his work in the railway and in the movement. During this time he had the joy of taking part in Paris's liberation and saw the arrival of the first tanks of Général Leclerc's heroic army.

Before this sad happening which caused the loss of the lives of so many of our brave friends I took part in quite a number of more or less important missions: sabotage, parachutings and transport of documents or receiving and emitting wireless sets.

The main items on the sabotage programme were important road, bridges, electrical transmitters and generators and railroads. As to this last object the work was rendered easy by the enemy and the then French government themselves. Every man was obliged to take his turn in patrolling a certain part of the railroads under the orders of a newly instituted special police of roads and highways. Certain of these officials, above all those in higher ranks, were very conscientious but the generality were far from being duty-struck. Many of them knew the "maquis" while others simply did not care. The men who were thus obliged to take part in the patrols came to know every inch of the tracks and the dangerous hours for a sabotage squad so they were of great help. I took part in a few of these expeditions but as the most important operations did not take place until D day and afterwards I never saw any really worthwhile. The most important I saw was the cutting of lines to hinder the arrival of troops while the "maquis" looted a siding in a small station or attacked a depot by surprise.

Receiving parachutings was always a source of joy to us all. I felt sometimes a little homesick on seeing the planes after turning around a few times go off homeward bound. These operations had to be conducted very rapidly. As soon as the aircraft had been directed over the site and the signals given, our trucks had to be ready. If the night was not too windy (I only saw one parachuting in full daylight and it was on the 14th July, 1944) and the airmen conscientious enough, the containers fell almost together and not very far away from one another but sometimes certain containers were a mile apart. We had to work rapidly because of the Germans or the French militia who, if they were near, heard the noise of aircraft. On the other hand one was never sure because of spies and traitors. There were certain cases where the enemy was at the parachuting site before the résistance" or where they arrived just in time to pick up the spoils after a brief running battle with our men who had not even the slightest chance against them. After one of these missions towards the end of September 1943 we had quite a scare. During the night we had received a good deal of arms, munitions and, above all, of explosives. Prior to distributing them to two different camps we had brought everything to a deserted country house near a small village and after hiding the two trucks had emptied the containers and verified the whole in the underground wine cellar. We had then retired to the loft where there was some straw to take some rest while one man remained on guard. We were nine in the loft. Shortly after daybreak we were awakened by the chief who recommended strict silence. From below we heard the unmistakable sound of German boots in the courtyard and in the house. An enemy column had stopped on the road just in front of our hiding place. If they searched the house and, above all, the cellar we were doomed. For an hour which seemed an eternity we waited almost motionless, our arms at the ready, decided to die fighting. But the attack never came. The column had apparently been in a hurry. They had stopped for breakfast. While the men were eating on the roadside the officers had been served in the abandoned house on an old rickety table, the only piece of furniture to be seen. Happily we had eaten in the cellar because had they seen any traces of a freshly eaten meal they would have searched everywhere. But if our doom had seemed certain to us they would not have come out of the engagement unscathed. After their departure we found our friend who had been on guard standing beside one of the biggest, home-made, white plastic bombs I have ever seen. Is was ready with detonator and rapid cord and could have blown half the village up as well as the house. His explanation was that he had only had time to warn the chief by an animal call and had gone to the cellar to make sure that if they found anything they would not have it free. If we were to die they would keep us company. The most important parachuting and the most encouraging I assisted at was the receiving at a few miles from the most important town of the central mountainous region of twenty American paratroopers with all their equipment comprising even two mortars. We certainly made them welcome as the forerunners of our liberators. (August 1944.)

Carrying documents or radio sets over long distances was always very interesting although exceedingly risky. The interest came from the fact that one felt one was doing something worthwhile. However there was a perpetual danger because of constant raids by the Germans or the French militia. Even if one went out for a five minute walk in the streets of a town occupied by the enemy (as they all were from November 1942) one was never sure of returning home. A main thoroughfare would be quite peaceful. Shoppers and others would be looking after their usual occupations. All of a sudden at certain points the street would be closed by enemy troops appearing seemingly from nowhere, young men and women would be herded into trucks and never seen or heard of again. They went to swell the army of German munition workers and many never came home again. I was once caught in one of these raids and only succeeded in escaping thanks to the kindness of a young shop assistant who allowed me to pass through the premises and through a back door into a side street. It was really a reign of terror. People could not go to a cinema or even to church without fear of German trucks which often awaited them at the door when the film or ceremony was ended. Travellers in trains were submitted to the same ignominious treatment both during the journey and in the stations because both papers and luggage were examined and the searchers did not need much of an excuse to make an arrest. The French militia were even more brutal and exacting than the Germans themselves.

At the beginning of May 1944 I had been asked to go to a certain town not very far from the Mediterranean coast to have certain papers which I was told were very important. I cannot say exactly what they contained but judging from our chief's manner of speaking of them they were very necessary. I was accompanied by Pierre, a fellow nurse in the hospital who had surprised me one morning – I was in a hurry putting my revolver in my mattress – but who was very discreet and reliable. He had very often helped me to get into the hospital in the small hours of the morning without being noticed. However he knew none of my secrets and had no idea of the identity of the members of the organisation or of our meeting places. The mission had passed off uneventfully. The person who was to bring the message had been long in coming, a whole week in fact. We could not wait so long in a hotel without having some occupation because the enemy was always on the look-out for seemingly idle people. About two or three miles outside the town was a monastery. We decided to ask to be accepted as guests there and were very well received. Each day at a certain time we went to the same place in the town and after a few uneventful days we at last saw the sign. The papers in our possession we left the next morning. Towards ten o'clock in the evening we arrived at the main station where we were to take the slow local train to our destination only to discover that we were too late for it and had to wait until six o'clock the next morning. It was both useless and dangerous to try to look for a room in a hôtel, useless because most of them were completely occupied by the Germans, dangerous because night patrols gathered up all young people on the streets even with regular papers. We decided to try to snatch a little sleep in the crowded waiting room and were just settling down when shortly after midnight the doors flew open and a dozen militiamen, Tommy-guns at the ready, burst in shouting: “All men on your feet with hands above your head.” I was half asleep but soon brought to my feet by the none too polite prod of a Tommy-gun on my chest. Cases and packets were brutally opened and examined. Papers were examined in detail. The documents I was carrying were in the lining of my small attaché case and happily were not found. Old women’s shawls and bonnets were torn off and examined in the most boisterous fashion. I made a remark to one of the younger militiamen (he was about seventeen years of age) about his impoliteness to an old lady of over seventy years of age who was sitting beside me. In reply he pushed his Tommy-gun into my stomach and threatened to arrest me. Happily their chief was at hand. I walked over to him and, very politely, explained the situation. On his tunic were seven or eight ribbons won in the last war. He asked to see my papers. Seeing I had been in the armistice army he said that he would not arrest a voluntary soldier but told me to be more careful what I said in future. However I breathed more freely when after arriving at the hospital I had given up the papers.

Time went on and days and weeks passed quickly. We knew that the “great day” could not be far away. It came more suddenly than ever I thought. One

Sunday afternoon in the middle of May 1944 the dentist's motorcycle came up to the hospital. On meeting him the smile on his face told me that something unusual had happened. In a few words he told me that on Monday I had to join the "maquis" in a small country place a few miles away. He would take me there. The leaders had already gone to prepare everything. After fixing the details of our rendezvous he left me overjoyed.

The moment for direct action had at last come. It was now "neck or nothing". To keep the hospital clear of all suspicion only one other should know and that was Pierre. Our last meeting for quite a time was full of true friendship. I felt that this time I was going away for good. There would be fighting and dangerous fighting so this quiet evening was lie a "veilleé d'armes". We both sat silent most of the time and our thoughts took their own ways.

The next morning I was awake early. My kit made ready the night before was far from voluminous: a small attaché case and a haversack. Quietly I left the hospital by the back way and down through the rocks I made my way to the railroad whose every sleeper I knew by heart all along this four and a half miles stretch. The walk was uneventful. Towards ten o'clock I arrived at the little town and, taking the usual path through the garden I arrived at Robert's house as agreed. After a good substantial meal I arose and, after saying goodbye to my friend's family, took my belongings and went down with Robert to the garage. On passing through the big entry I saw three or four of the road police in the street. It would not have been any trouble for my friend to take the motorcycle out as he was a surgeon dentist and had a special permit but it could have seemed suspect that he had a pillion rider with an attaché case and a haversack and who, more important that all, carried a loaded revolver and spare ammunition. To save any trouble I arranged with his friend to walk on with the almost empty haversack. Robert took the small case behind him and promised to meet me in about half an hour. I struck out gaily, saluting here and there a friend but keeping my eyes open in case I might meet German soldiers or a militia patrol who asked for papers but who also very often searched especially young men. I was quite ready to let my gun fall into one of the hedges which bordered the main road and separated it from the fields on either side and for that purpose kept it in my hand in the right jacket pocket. This was the only solution because to engage upon a lone fight in such flat land as was made by the fields each side of the road would be sheer nonsense. A little more than a mile from the town near the beginning of another little agglomeration the road wound up under an archway of poplars turning a bend. Here I found myself face to face with one of the local members of the road police. "Where are you off to with your haversack and your heavy boots Maurice?" he asked. "Oh, I'm off to try to find some butter and eggs or anything in that line in the farms round about to make a spread for the chums at the hospital." The official was not on duty and so continued to talk away. I tried to walk on but the other did not seem in a hurry so I had to make the best of it. Suddenly I heard in the distance the noise of a motorcycle. As they were not very numerous on the road I was almost sure it was Robert who was already on his way and mentally swore at this unlucky happening. Sure enough a few seconds later Robert came flashing past on his machine and, on seeing me, pulled up quickly. Making a big circle in the road he came back to where I stood with the annoying official. "How are you Maurice?" said he. "Very well thank you, M. Dupré. Are you off to the hospital today?" "Oh no," he said, "Why?" "Because I would have asked for a lift for a mile or so as I am going into the country to look for some provisions and you could have carried me to the crossroads." Robert replied that he was going to a small village to see a client and suggested that should begin my provision hunt there. After saying how lucky I was the official left us. I strapped my case on my back and we were on our way. After a quick ride through a beautiful wooded country we arrived in the quiet little town where we were to meet the liaison agent, a butcher, who was to bring us to the "maquis". The shop was halfway down the main street. We stopped a little further on near a garage to avoid suspicion and I went into the shop where I saw a young shop assistant and a middle-aged lady. I approached the latter and, while speaking about the weather, gave the password. The effect was instantaneous. I was shown into the back shop where I met the boss. On learning that I was not alone he bade me call Robert and together we made our way to the butcher's home a few yards away where we were very well received. After an excellent refreshment we were told to go to the garage near which Robert had left his motorcycle, give the password and await our new comrade's arrival. Everything went off smoothly and in an hour's time an old car was ready to take us to our destination. The proprietor, a middle-aged man, was to bring us. The old car seemed quite good and its owner was very good company. We got in and soon were on route for our destination.

Amid a joyous but casual conversation the motor rolled along the main road. After about six miles, which brought us to the county limit, the car wheeled off to the right taking a side road large enough for a car or even for a truck. On the left it was bordered by a hedgerow but on the right by a thick undergrowth which climbed up quite a steep slope to meet a thick pine wood. The driver began to give queer sounds with the klaxon and I began to realise that we had almost arrived. The heavy undergrowth suddenly gave way to a clearing and the car stopped quite abruptly. "Here you are." said the driver as he opened the door and stepped out. Both of us were astonished that nobody came to greet us. The chauffeur gave us our belongings and said "Take the first little path on the right. I am not supposed to go into the wood but you will certainly meet someone. I don't think that the camp is very far in." Before going any further I had a good look around me. The place was certainly ideally well chosen. The clearing was elliptical, about two hundred yards long and at its longest point seventy-five yards wide. The slope from the road was rather abrupt. "Fine place." said I. "The greeting seems quite cold, I suppose we must go to meet them if they won't come to us." Together we began climbing the slope and soon arrived in front of a narrow, beaten path wide enough to allow only one man to pass at a time. We had scarcely advanced three yards when the black muzzle of a Tommy-gun jutted forth from behind a young tree and a stern, business-like voice ordered us to halt. We did so and a man of about thirty years of age emerged from behind the tree and asked for the password. "Saint Angèle," said I. "What is your business here?" he said. I then told him that Lieutenant X had told me to come to this relay camp pending my passage to a fighting unit. He lowered his arm to allow me to pass but as Robert made to accompany me he abruptly stopped him. "I'm sorry, sir, but you must go back." I explained my friend's situation and all the help he had given us but the sentry remained adamant. Every persuasion failed. "I cannot allow him to pass. Even our friend who brought you here never comes up to the camp." I began to feel a little annoyed but seeing myself powerless was preparing to say goodbye to my friend when a voice which I easily recognised as that of the lieutenant in charge and whom I had frequently met in the company of D.14 floated down to us. "What's wrong, Réne?" "Come down lieutenant." cried the sentry. A few seconds later our fair-haired smiling young friend arrived with a very alarming Thompson repeater under his arm. When he saw us he greeted us warmly and I explained the trouble. He then became a little worried. "The orders are very severe. We must not let any strangers to the camp into the inside. You know how important it is for us that nobody should be able to "squeal" even under torture and you know how the Militia and Gestapo can do it. We never allow any of the boys to go back home from here unless their previous activity has given us very good reasons to have confidence in them. These days we are very worried because five days ago while on a sabotage mission one of our boys was rather stupidly taken prisoner by the Militia. He was never very courageous and it is very probable that he will talk. So you see, Robert, you had better not come to the camp. I am sorry but if you like to wait a few minutes we shall have a glass of wine before saying goodbye. Give us your water-bottle Réné. I will fill it up for you later." We all drank with joy out of the same tin cup because it was very warm and then we accompanied Robert, who went sorrowfully downhill back to the car which was to bring him back to civil life.

After a heartfelt farewell we again took the road to the wood. I felt that a new life had begun for me and that I was going to have the occasion to "do my bit". We passed the sentry who had never left his post. Lieutenant X took his water-bottle "for a refill" of wine and we made our way through a labyrinth of paths to a clearing where a really comforting sight met my eyes. Seven long huts made of short pine trees interwoven with branches were built at regular intervals. Each one bore the name of famous African battles and the centre one that of Bin-Harkin where the French had made their glorious stand. The roof of this hut was extended and on a table under this shelter was a most comforting display of automatic arms and munitions. One thing however surprised me and that was the absence of men. I asked the lieutenant where everybody was because as all I could see was five others I expected that some were on missions and others on guard. I was quite astonished when he explained that all together we were only ten. Three of the most reliable were on sentry duty, one hear at the entrance of the country road, one at the entrance to the camp which we had taken and the other at the opposite end of the country road near the other main road which was about ten minutes away. He explained that he was pleased that I had come because of the danger brought about by the captivity of one of the boys a few days previously as he had already told Robert and I and because, as I could see, three of the young boys were about fifteen to seventeen years of age and were only learning how to handle a gun. They had never been in a dangerous corner before. This lieutenant had been obliged to send off a convoy of eighty that very morning because he had to profit of the numbers available in order to satisfy the fighting units who were in great need of men. He asked me to second him in case of attack saying that the knowledge of my nationality would galvanise the others and give them confidence in what would be certainly a heavy fight. The presentation proved the truth of his supposition and I was unanimously adopted.

On visiting the camp I had to admire the organisation. Every hut could hold thirty to forty men and was well supplied with straw (each one brought a blanket). There was plenty of food and ammunition, enough for at least fifty men to hold out for an hour or two. It was really amazing to think that from the outside no one would ever suspect the existence of such an organisation. The rest of the afternoon was passed in preparing and distributing arms and ammunition and in giving orders in case of surprise. I was to take sentry post at the opposite edge of the country road which fringed the wood. The lieutenant was to take the other extremity while another was to guard the approach from the clearing. The experienced men who already held these posts were to take command of the younger men in case of attack. In this case we were all to close in, still fighting near the edge of the belt to bring the enemy into the clearing in which position we could hold quite long and be near our munitions. If we were outnumbered we were to strike off into the thickness of the wood and follow its two and a half miles crescent into a swampy part known by all except myself where we would probably not be followed. When everything was clearly understood (it was astonishing how these men without uniforms understood discipline when they were in danger but out of this circumstance did not want to understand it) the lieutenant and myself left the wood, took to the cart track and, our Tommy-guns over our arm, six full charges in our belt and a grenade in each pocket, went towards the sentry's post which was to be mine until morning. It was about 7.30 p.m. and we were walking slowly conversing on one thing and another. The lieutenant was telling me about the two radio messages which had already come through and how all were awaiting the third which was to announce the Allied landing in Europe. The "maquis" expected that soon after a massive airborne landing would come to them in the centre of France to organise and help them to partake efficiently in the chasing of the hated Germans.

Conversing thus we arrived near the end of the road and, as it was not yet quite daylight, we looked to where the sentry was. Quite surprised at his absence the lieutenant called softly, "Marco, where are you?" No reply. Our astonishment deepened and the lieutenant repeated his call a little louder this time. "Psst," was the only reply. We looked in the direction of the undergrowth and there was Marco with his arm at the ready. "Come quickly and watch out…" He had not time to finish. A rattle of automatic fire which made the turf spit up around us and chops of bark with pieces of branches sing past our ears interrupted us. I threw myself flat, wriggled well under cover and turned round to face the enemy as quickly as I could. Two light cars, Bren-guns through the windscreen and the side windows flew past, firing as they came. A truck carrying blue-uniformed militiamen followed. This had happened like a streak of lightning and I scarcely had time to put a charge into my Thompson but when I heard the roar of another truck I took aim at the entrance of the country road. In a whirlwind of dust the second truck arrived but did not go far. I emptied a full charge into its windscreen at about fifteen-yard range. As it was just turning the truck reeled like a ship in a heavy sea and finished its course with its front wheels in the deep ditch and its motor still running. The militias jumped out but I had the presence of mind to throw a hand grenade. I do not know whether it landed where I wished or not because a blinding flash which I learned later had been caused by one of Marco's grenades almost blinded me. My projectile burst a second or two afterwards and we were almost blinded by these two detonations and the earth they threw up. It was only later that I saw the damage done. A third truck arrived only to pile itself upon what was left of the other. The most important was how to rejoin the camp because we could hear the rattle of musketry coming from there. All this had happened in the space of a few seconds which had seemed very long but we knew that it was most urgent to rejoin the camp as soon as possible. Keeping as near the edge of the wood as safety would allow we raced on, stopping every few seconds to empty a few rounds into the hedge on the other side of the cart track behind which we could see the moving shadows of the survivors of the second and third trucks who logically were endeavouring to rejoin their more fortunate comrades. Our stratagem we realised later had a double result: bring the enemy into a very disadvantageous position and give them as impression of force, both things essential for our success and safety. On arriving at the top of the crest in the middle of the clearing we found that René (the sentry who had stopped Robert and I) had not lost any time. While firing a good number of Tommy-gun salvos he had quickly retreated towards the interior of the wood in the direction of the camp and, to the tune of two hand grenades to dissuade any temporary militia charge, had rallied the five others and sent for a Bren-gun which one of the young boys and Jeannot, one of the older hands, were putting into position. The lieutenant's orders were short but precise: "Maurice take the Bren with the two youngsters to fill your chargers and use a few grenades if necessary. Marco take his right and you Jeannot his left while the lads bring more ammunition and hand grenades. When they come back spread out on either side to keep your eyes on each side of the crescent; keep moving to let them think we are more numerous. If they try to get into the wood from either side you know our tactics: Save all the arms and munitions you can but no foolishness. I am going down to meet Pierre who is near the other road in case this might be only the first episode. That stupid little… must have talked."

The enemy seemed to have overcome their surprise and began firing continuously. Their Bren bullets whispered dangerously near. It was my "baptism du feu" in the maquis but I really enjoyed it. I had no time to think. Just as I was settling down and getting to know my gun the enemy fire doubled in intensity. Three successive explosions shook the hedge and from the openings this made under cover of an extremely heavy fire they tried to reach the cover of the wood on either horn of the crescent. But they did not go far. They had to climb so we had the advantage. Marco and René seemed like those eastern gods to have numberless hands. Grenades and gunfire seemed literally to pour on the assailants. We learned the reason later and the lieutenant and the other sentry from the end of the road by which Robert and I had arrived had come to the rescue and by frequent short displacements had given the impression of quite a great armed force. The militia turned back leaving several dead and wounded on the field. Several had been hit and had gone limping away. They kept sniping at us but we only fired when we saw a target. Now and again I fired a few rounds into and over the hedgerow in as wide a range as the two ends of the wood allowed me because I was not sure of the positions taken by the others and did not want to touch them. All of a sudden we heard some heavy firing coming simultaneously from both horns of the crescent. The French traitors were attacking from both sides but were being well received. How our chums had managed to guess what was going to happen I do not yet know but there seemed to be some on each side and the militia had not everything their own way. The centre seemed quiet so I decided to see what was going on farther down. The two adolescents who were with me had not enough experience to be of great help and I was mostly afraid of their being reckless. In a few words I explained to the older of them the mechanism of my Bren. The other knew how to fill the chargers. If ever the weapon jammed they must retreat with it to the camp and, after hiding it in the fork of a tree or somewhere like that await, duly armed and ever on the look-out, until someone came for them. Above all there must be no panic. This settled and understood I went down to the right, my Tommy-gun at the ready, full chargers in my belt and four grenades hanging from my body belt at the back. I went cautiously from tree to tree eyes and ears wide open. I had not gone very far when chips of bark began to fly around me. I had not realised that the shooting was so near and redoubled attention. Still jumping from tree to tree I continued to advance when about five yards in front I saw a dark form moving. After stopping I noticed that it was coming slowly backwards, firing sparingly. On a more careful scrutiny I realised that it was Marco. My situation was quite dangerous: I must not surprise him because he would shoot immediately so

I continued going carefully from trunk to trunk until I was opposite him and only separated from him by about three yards. From there I called him and he quickly turned both his head and his weapon. When he had identified me he smiled and in a bound was beside me. "I am running short of ammunition. René is a little over to the right. I have given him all I could and am on my way to have some more. They are gaining ground on this side. The others who are nearer the camp over there seem to be holding better. If the d… traitors realise how few we are we are lost. Keep 'em going I won't be long but watch your step. They have not advanced but might try a rush. Use your grenades. We might not have to fight long for the sun is going down." With a warm handshake he ran off.

Carefully, making use of every cover, I crept forward. Now and again a salvo of automatic gunfire ploughed up the shrubbery. Farther down, on my right, Réné seemed to be holding his own. From the other side the fighting seemed intense. All of a sudden I heard subdued voices and peering through the bushes saw not far away several of the hated navy blue uniforms. Slowly unhitching a grenade from behind my back I pulled the pin, held the lever tight and advancing as far as safety would allow, got up on one knee and threw it. From where I was lying on my face the ground shook. I jumped up almost at once, advanced a few yards, threw another and fell flat. The shrubs shook with the explosion which was accompanied and followed by yells and curses. To continue the effect I made another jump forward and threw my third explosive. Afterwards there was a silence, rather ominous, and punctuated by groans. I wished to proceed to see what had been the result of my tactics but realised that I had better not. It was lucky for me that I did not move, two grenades burst in succession a little below me. I answered them with my last and prepared myself for the rush which never came. A Bren began to sweep my area but well sheltered behind two big pine trees I was in safety. I answered with sparing salvos from my Tommy-gun always moving but keeping undercover. The sun was going down and it was becoming quite dusk. In the undergrowth darkness comes quickly and before long the shadows were deepening. The enemy had quietened down really too much for me and so I decided to retreat slowly towards the camp. A shadow on my right made me jump but is was René. I was so pleased to see him. Marco, who had not been very far behind me and had thought that the hand grenade explosions had been the beginning of the militia's attack, joined us. How happy we were to be together again all safe and sound. For a few seconds we forgot our perilous situation and, almost unable to speak, hugged one another. All of a sudden a heavy burst of Bren-gun firing interrupted us. "The youngsters are fighting," I cried and we broke into a run. On reaching the post we were delighted to see the two boys, their eyes trying to pierce the dusk, literally watering the hedgerow at the bottom of the slope. "We saw shadows behind it and are doing our bit," said the gunner. We clapped him on the back and waited for the next move. Except for a few salvos farther and farther away along the country road everything was quiet. "They have gone," sighed Marco, "but happily not all. Some of them won't be home tonight." In the distance motor engines throbbed. "Why didn't they blow up the cars and trucks?" cried one of the adolescents. "First of all they had not much time and secondly it would have been a great mistake," said the experienced Marco. "Had they done so the militia would have gone to the nearest telephone to send for a conveyance and help. We would have been surrounded and attacked by an overwhelming force round about dawn. As it is they will go for reinforcements and only be back sometime tomorrow. The camp is now known so we may have no scruples in abandoning it after hiding all the munitions and arms. Tomorrow our camp will be inexistent. They will attack a few huts in an empty wood. Jeannot and René have a look for the lieutenant and the others; we are going to hide everything."

We had been working more than half an hour when Jeannot and René came back and by the worried look on their faces we expected the worst; "No sign of any of them," sighed René "only a few bodies of militiamen down there." "They have perhaps been taken prisoners," said I. "I don't think so," replied Marco, "they are too experienced for anything like that to happen to them. I am sure they are still prowling around somewhere. The lieutenant knows his way about here more than anyone else. We must not worry too much about them. As you did not discover their bodies I feel quite safe about them. We must finish hiding our material and get out of here in case of surprise because this time it will be no joke and we must keep our lives and strength for a more useful day." We accepted his advice and an hour later only the abandoned huts remained of so fine an installation. Under Marco's orders, we had unanimously and tacitly accepted his leadership, we filed off through the woods in the direction of the town. It was very dark and we walked quickly but cautiously in an Indian file behind our new chief.

Alone I would have had great difficulty in finding my way through the wood and especially through the very swampy plain which separated it from the town but following thus a so sure leader it was easy. Armed as we were we felt quite sure of ourselves. When we arrived on the main road at about half a mile from the town we advanced more cautiously. However everything seemed quiet. We were all quite tired after our fight and our walk through the woods. On the outskirts of the town we found a big open shed and as it was quite cold (we were at about seven hundred metres) we lay down in the most sheltered corner and snuggling together for warmth we tried to rest. Marco and Jeannot went off to see what was going on in the town and half an hour later came back with four big bottles of wine and the explanation of the attack. The Panther (a very beautiful blonde and one of the occupying army's most dreaded spies, had been in the district two days before. One of the boys from the camp had been seen with her the day after her arrival. We guessed the rest because she always traded her charms, and usually very successfully, for information. We were pleased that the boy who had been taken prisoner a few days before seemed thus not the cause but we made the resolution to find the culprit in the advanced camp he had gone to and let him know the result of his folly.

While we were enjoying our wine we were rudely awakened to our dangerous situation by the sound of a motor car. Everything at the ready we hid behind the carts in the shed. A black motor car swung rapidly past. It was alone and seemed to stop near the centre of the little town. "Keep your eyes open. I will go and see what is going on," said Marco and, before anyone could stop him he slipped out into the night leaving all his arms behind him. Tensely we waited. Our tiredness had left us and we were prepared for anything. In a few minutes the noise of the motor began again and soon we saw the headlights coming in front of our hiding-place. A hearty chuckle and Marco's rich voice chimed out "Don't shoot lads, it's only me." It was one of the organisation's motor cars used for convoy work and its two occupants had just come back from their journey with the men who had left the camp in the morning for the hills. After learning from Marco what had happened the convoy chief told us that we must leave there the next day. He brought us all into a little cottage where an elderly old lady who called us all "son" gave us a very comfortable and replenishing hot supper. I asked where all the food came from as restrictions were so severe but the chief told me that he looked after that and saw to it all. "Now you must all have a good rest." he said, "You will have quite a trying day tomorrow. I cannot offer you any comfortable bed but you will have to make the best of it." After bidding good-night to our so kind and venerable hostess we made our way across the little town to a farm. Everyone seemed to be in bed but a few pebbles thrown against a window soon brought a light and a man's head: "I'll be down immediately." said he in reply to our chief's greeting. In a few minutes a middle-aged farmer came down and led us behind his home into a big barn full of hay. "Here is your hôtel," said the chief. The farmer showed us a way of getting out in case of emergency and asking us not to smoke for fear of fire bade us good-night and went back to bed. We snuggled down in the hay feeling tired out. Soon I heard the heavy breathing around me. All were off to sleep. I was feeling fagged out myself but with the day's emotions I could not sleep. For a certain time I lay thinking of my new life and wondering how it would end but soon sleep overtook me and I sank into oblivion.

I awakened next morning with the crowing of the farmyard cocks. They must have been crowing quite a time because the sun seemed high. Jeannot was already awake and smoking a cigarette out of the little window which should have served as an emergency exit. As soon as he heard me stirring he turned and after wishing me good-morning asked me if I had had a good night. "Let's wake the others and go back to camp to see what has been going on. I am still worried about the lieutenant and the other." We awakened then and I asked suddenly "Where is Marco?" "He has gone out into the town to see if all is clear. He will be back any minute now." He had scarcely finished speaking down our improvised leader came in with a jug of steaming coffee and a tin cup. "Come on lads, we must be off. Everything is quiet." After our hasty breakfast and a word of thanks to the farmer we made off in the direction of the camp. It was a beautiful morning and after a good night's rest we were all in quite high spirits. On the way we chatted gaily, happy to think that if all went well we would be with a more important and more active unit in the evening. Everything went well until we arrived at about a mile from the camp. In a little clearing beside a ruined farmhouse stood, with their backs to us, two men. Marco, who was in the lead as usual made a sign for us to take cover and, after advancing a few yards, uttered a loud laugh and called for us to come on. We went forward to find the liaison agent who had directed me to the camp and another friend of the "Résistance" was awaiting us with unbelievable news. The third message had come through and, what was better, the Allies had officially landed round the Normandy coast. The situation was a little confused but one thing was certain, they were there and that was the most important. The idea of their not succeeding never entered our minds. We hugged one another in joy. Then all of a sudden we remembered the lieutenant and the others. What had become of them. The chief informed us with a smile that they had followed the militia until they were sure they had really gone and had then come back to bury the dead who the enemy in their retreat had not ventured to gather up as they were too much in the open. They were worrying about us just as much as we were about them he assured us and after telling us to have a rest said that we must stand by to await the coming in the evening of means of conveyance to go to join the fighting units. Congratulating and warning us to be careful he left us. We continued and soon gained the camp where our lost friends had prepared us a good breakfast.

About ten o'clock our convoy friends who had saved us the night before arrived and began giving instructions. At mid-day the ammunition and all the arms were ready and a truck arrived giving us quite a fright. After a good meal we took our positions in the truck: two with the Bren-gun over the driver's cabin, another Bren with gunman and servant at the back, the others with their arms and grenades at the ready. Beside the driver was Marco with a real arsenal. The light car preceding us, our modest convoy got underway at about two o'clock in the afternoon. The tactics were simple and easy to carry out. The light car was to carry on ahead of us. At every crossroads it was to do a certain distance up each road and be back at the crossing to give us the "all clear" or otherwise. If it met a German or militia "barrage" it was, if possible, to come back and warn us, if impossible, to accept battle so that the firing would warn us. We were to help them if we could. If they heard us fighting they were to come to help us. In any case, come what may, we were not to leave the truck without orders and in that case to try to keep together as much as the circumstances would allow. However the journey passed off quietly. It took us four long hours to arrive at our destination, four hours of joyous greeting from every village we passed through and from every person we met. The Allied landing was known and people were all in great joy. I only had one thrill during that long ride: a few miles from our camp I was taking my turn as gunman at the Bren above the driver's cabin. Everything had been going well. All of a sudden I saw at a turning the convoy car had stopped before a gendarmerie office and four or five gendarmes were around it. I shouted a warning which brought the lieutenant up beside me at full speed. He began to laugh. "If the 'boys' have stopped beside them it must be O.K." I was not so sure because I had learned to have very little confidence in them unless I knew them perfectly so I kept my hands on the gun even when we were drawing alongside the small in. Our convoy chief came out of the car quite worried. The Germans and a militia group were on the move not far off and we could not take another road. We could not depend too much on our speed as the country was very hilly (we were at about 900 metres above sea level and were going up to over 1100) The gendarmes were very good. They had telephoned to many of their posts on our route but there was no sure news. It was from this day onwards that my bad opinion of the gendarmes disappeared. I was to see the proofs of the double activity of many who had the liberty given them by their uniform for the good of the "Résistance". In spite of this bad news however we decided to carry on. There could be no question of going back (our camp was now known) and we were supposed to meet the other small convoy a little more than halfway. Certain individuals were also to be picked up on the way. So we continued replying to all the wholehearted good wishes showered upon us in every hamlet and village but keeping eyes and ears open to the utmost. Coming near the dangerous point we felt a little unsafe but soon everything was over. The gendarmerie posts and the little country post offices gave us the "all clear". It was really a great relief because we were not in a position (numerical or otherwise) to fight in the open. It became cold because we were climbing constantly and the country was becoming wilder and wilder.

About half-past four we arrived at the small town where we were to meet the other convoy. What a welcome! The flags were out in spite of the fact that the Germans had passed there just a few hours earlier. A small convoy awaited us, two trucks and a "scout" car. The occupants were mainly dressed in air force uniforms. Where they came from I did not know but they all seemed familiar to the people who were there to give us a great send-off. Wine was flowing fast and most of our new comrades were, if not drunk, very nearly so. The French flag flew from each of the trucks and it was to the strain of their songs that we started off again. It became decidedly colder, the country more and more savage and mountainous and I realised that we were nearing our journey's end. But the trucks rolled on only stopping at certain points where the convoy cars had stopped before us in order to telephone to assure us against any surprise. At several of the stops we picked up a few young men each with his pack over his shoulders bubbling over with the news of the Allied landing and giving the latest details of the BBC. Soon we began crossing other trucks marked F.F.1. who cheered us on our way and all of a sudden the convoy stopped dead at one of the wildest and lost deserted parts of the road we had yet seen. After about a quarter of an hour our convoy chief came out of a side road which was, so to speak, only visible to vehicles coming from the opposite direction. He made a sign and our trucks entered into it one by one because no two cars could ride abreast. The going was very bad and we had to hold on like grim death. About a hundred yards down we passed an outpost: two Brens and a section of about ten or fifteen men. Not far down was another. A little farther a bracken hut seemed to be the HQ of the post. We continued our rocky way until about a mile down we came upon a clearing with the wood on our right and a big field on the left. This field seemed to serve as car park because between cars and trucks of various kinds and sizes there were about at least fifty vehicles. We were told to leave the trucks and with our lieutenant at the head we followed the country road until we came to a little hamlet not far off. Here we were ordered to go on to another place whose name I did not understand. After more than half an hour's trudging through woods and across fields we reached our goal which was a decent sized country farmhouse and the camp's GHQ.

On the way I had noticed many similar places occupied by young men in uniform with navy blue beret, brown leather blouse, brown shorts. At GHQ I was to learn that after the enlistment groups were sent off to these different places for instructions and training. I took my place in the queue in front of the "office" (a table under the spreading branches of a big tree). In my pocket was my passport and my false French identity card. While awaiting my turn I was very astonished to see that the officers in charge of the enlistment asked for no identity papers. They gave each one the choice of giving his real name or his "nom de guerre" (in any case a "nom de guerre" had to be chosen for one's own safety) I felt a little uneasy in this atmosphere. Where was the strict secrecy of the "Résistance" groups I had known? "Of course," I said to myself, "all these men must have been sent here by underground organisations who knew them." However I felt that there was something wrong somewhere. When my turn came I decided to play straight because as my family knew nothing about my whereabouts I wanted to be sure that they would be informed if anything happened to me. When I announced my name the officers and those directly beside me looked at me in surprise. Thereupon I produced my passport. Immediately I felt a certain suspicion and hostility. Instead of being sent to the same company as my comrades I was told to stay at the GHQ to exercise my profession as a male nurse. I asked no questions but went simply to the big barn above the house (in that region the farmhouse is usually built against a height so that the hay carts which are smaller and narrower than those regularly in use in this country can, by using this slope, go into the barn above the house to discharge the hay so precious during the winter for the cattle which form the almost sole income of the Auvergnat peasant). Here I looked for a free corner and a little straw to have a well-earned rest. The evening passed quickly.

Two more convoys arrived and there was a great deal of animation. Supper time came at about seven o'clock and we had quite a good meal. Meat, butter, sugar, etc. seemed plentiful. Everyone in our section seemed in good spirits. I took a quiet walk around to see what the place looked like but had a vague impression that I was being followed. Everywhere I went a middle-aged man who wore the signs of company sergeant-major was not far behind me. The next day my suspicions were confirmed. Convoys were still arriving. Our number was increasing and as I had nothing to do I mixed with the new arrivals asking for fresh news of the Allied progress in France. There was nothing very special but the most important was that they were holding. As I mingled with the groups of newcomers I was conscious of being followed. At last I decided to have things cleared up. To make sure once more that I was not making a mistake I purposely went from one little group to another exchanging only a few remarks here and there and my suspicions were once more confirmed: from one group to another my "shadow" followed me. I turned to him suddenly. "Why are you following me about? Do you wish to speak to me, to ask me something? If there is anything wrong please tell me." He seemed embarrassed. "Are you really English? (for them all the inhabitants of the British Isles were Englishmen). On my affirmative reply he blurted out rather bluntly and with a suspicious look on his face, "You are a member of the Intelligence

Service?" I answered with a laugh that I had not that honour but he did not seem convinced. Seeing his reaction I was really hurt because I had the feeling I was to have more than once later, namely that certain inferior chiefs in the movement objected to British interference in their affairs and were always inclined to be suspicious of anything seemingly "English". Their seeming reasons I only found out later on. Understanding his disbelief of my statement I explained in a few words what I had come through to be where I was and how, speaking perfect French, having regular French papers and having an occupation in such a quiet place as the hospital in which I had been employed I could have remained snugly out of danger instead of coming here. I made him understand that if I had been in contact with the Intelligence Service I would have had a much more interesting situation in the "Résistance". However he must have been quite satisfied because he left me and all through the evening I saw no more of him. I watched to see if someone else was taking his place but I could not spot anyone in particular.

I began to feel more at ease but the discovery of the mistrust had shaken me up a bit. The forced inactivity was very unpleasant and, what was more, I was struck by the lack of arms and munitions. While walking around the HQ (we were allowed about a mile radius around this part of the camp and the orders were quite severe; at this distance one invariably found sentries who barred the way to those who did not know the password) I saw several sections of young men who were doing exercise but very few were armed. If ever we are attacked, I thought, we shall never be able to hold. Many of those I met were very of my opinion and, above all, the older men who had taken part in the 1914-1918 was and the 1939-1940 campaign. And to make things worse more recruits kept flocking in by hundreds. Some were armed (e.g. police and gendarmes) but the majority was made up of youths who had absolutely no experience. And there was still the maddening absence of control with regards to identity or rank. With regard to the question of identity there was perhaps an excuse because, as I have said before, as each convoy generally came from a relay camp and as such was very liable to have been checked on leaving but rank is also a very important question in an irregular army where officers or NCOs are very valuable. Here all sorts of declarations were accepted and I felt that it was a bad omen (later I was to see that I was right). How was the camp to arm so many? If there was not a "cache" in the camp it was useless to keep so many men. That night we had not been long asleep when we were quickly awakened. A German column was in the district. News of its presence was sent by telephone to the outposts and from there to the HQ. We were quickly ready (few of us were undressed the barn being cold and our only bedding a handful of straw and a thin blanket) and marched out in a double file behind the NCOs with our officers in the lead. The road seemed long but in half an hour we were told to stop on a thickly- wooded hillside. It was rather ignominious for a "fighting unit". I had hoped for action but here we were fleeing before the enemy. After about two hours in the damp cold we were given the order to move off again and were soon back in the camp without incident. Early in the morning the sector was in movement. I was preparing myself for another day of idleness when the sergeant-major who had "shadowed" me the first day called on me to follow him to the lieutenant's office. On arriving there the officer explained in a few words his reasons for calling me. The night's alarm had been false. Someone who knew the ways of the camp had "tapped" the telephone line not far off. He had every reason to believe that the culprit was perhaps even in the camp. I was to have the freedom of the camp with the general password and was to watch the attitude or movements of all newcomers. I was not to hide my real nationality in the hope of enticing interesting conversations. My going about from section to section was to be covered by the fact that I was acting as liaison between HQ and the other parts of the camp. Needless to say I was only too happy to have an occupation.

My first day allowed me to see the state and construction of the camp. There were nearly four thousand men spread out in about fifteen little hamlets which had been expropriated or already abandoned when the camp was n way of organisation. Everyone seemed quite active. Section upon section was manoeuvring but it seemed to me, and later events were to prove it, that they were being taught according to an erroneous plan. The training was in view of ordinary warfare whereas our task was that of guerrillas, at least such was my former chief's way of considering the question. The enemy had tanks and heavy artillery while we had neither. Certain camps like those of High Savoy in the Alps where certain regiments of regular soldiers had retired with arms and equipment were able to withstand an attack or even, if regularly supplied, to stage even more positive tactics. But then what could a camp like this do in case of attack? There was neither arms nor munitions and men were flowing in every day. We had scarcely enough light automatic arms to furnish five hundred men for any considerable time. This shortage was really striking and most discouraging. There was much talk of a great parachutage of arms, munitions and uniforms which was to come any night and a cunningly hidden wireless post was permanently manned for the purpose of directing it. If this arrived it would certainly change the aspect of the camp a great deal. It was greatly needed because some of the young men who had already been in the camp three or four weeks had thin clothes in a pitiful state. The food question was well cared for and twice a week herds of cattle (more or less considerable) were brought from quite far off by men of the "maquis" slaughtered, skinned, prepared and divided among the various parts of the camp. But men kept pouring in and this problem must have been becoming really difficult. I wondered how the situation of the camp remained unknown by the enemy with all the movement converging towards it. It was really a mystery how such organisations could prevail in the conditions of the country at that time when one could trust nobody, even sometimes one's dearest and closest friend. On the whole the camp was well organised. There were even doctors and the officers often spoke of a field ambulance to be placed in a small hamlet outside of the camp. Because of my nursing experience I was expecting to go there in due time. Everything was well planned out, too well planned in fact because infinitely unpractical and with hopeless disregard for hard facts. There was penury of arms, munitions and uniforms. The camp was more than full of inexperienced men and every hour which followed D day saw more and more streaming in. Food had to be brought from afar and requisitioned in a country where rations were more than meagre. Livestock was a real problem because it had to be led from afar. Very often a small herd of some ten to twelve necessitated a three to four days march. Both men and beasts arrived in a very tired state because often they could only use the roads during night time. They could not be brought in motor vehicles because since D day the Germans had forbidden all motor circulation on the roads: they fired without warning on any such vehicle. It was only later that they allowed doctors' cars or food transport lorries to use the roads and the latter had to fly a very visible white flag, the former the international red cross. What was more, even if the men in the camp had been armed with the usual automatic arms they could never have withstood an enemy attack. There was a complete absence of artillery dispose of tanks, artillery, thousands of trained men. It was sheer folly to even think of trying to establish such a camp and. Above all, to give it even a slight appearance of permanency. Our hide-out would inevitably be discovered sooner or later. My impression was that the leaders had seen things on too big a scale. I learned also that the reason of the continued inflow of men was the fact that in the villages and small towns the local "résistance" chiefs were inciting everyone to "take to the maquis" and in certain cases were making it almost compulsory. It seemed to me that everyone was seeing things too big and there was a lack of co-ordination.

Another question gave me food for thought: why did the much-awaited and much-needed parachutage not come? There was, so I learned, two sources of supplies: Algiers and London. Why did neither of them send the so needed material? Were our chiefs (we had two commanders with rank of major, one civil who was the organiser of the camp and one military) really in contact with the higher command or had they undertaken this particular task of their own account? That they had been in the "résistance" I have no doubt but that on their own initiative they had gone as far as to organise these big camps (there were four in the region of the same size) was a very hazardous enterprise which cost lives and might have even cost many more. Whoever was at fault incurred very certainly a considerable responsibility. But I am anticipating the events. During my first day I saw nothing very worthy of attention. I came back in the evening for supper which took place about seven o'clock to learn that a big convoy from Montlucon had been ambushed by the militia and that there had been a few deaths. The survivors arrived with one quite badly wounded. One of his knees had been smashed by a bullet. When the doctor operated on him we took a twisted machine-gun bullet out of the articulation which was in a bad state. The operation was finished about 8.30 p.m. and as I was walking about smoking a last cigarette before turning in my friend the adjutant appeared suddenly alongside me and after a few commonplace remarks guided my steps towards a quiet part of the sector. An interesting subject had arrived with the last convoy. He seemed a great talker and knew by name most of the "résistance" chiefs of the region. He seemed to know a great deal about everything, spoke of his experience of "sabotage", etc. In brief he spoke too much about everything and asked too many questions. What was more serious he tried to talk with all those who had any rank whatsoever and before everyone he published his knowledge and experience. We decided to keep an eye on him seriously. He was tall, dressed in grey and seemed to be about thirty-five. He "turned in" with us in the big barn at HQ and the night passed uneventfully. Next day I decided to stay at HQ to keep an eye on our "suspect". After enrolment, the convoy had arrived a little late the night before, he was to stay with the "special" company which remained at HQ. He seemed very pleased with himself and strutted about conversing with all the officers and graded soldiers he could see. My friend, the sergeant-major, introduced him to me under my real name. From thence he never left me during the whole morning. His conversation was really very interesting but I had an unmistakable impression that he was looking for news. He reviewed the camp's situation with its possibilities and advantageous position with regards to retreat in case of attack. (His knowledge of the surroundings seemed perfect). To him everything seemed perfect but it was very easy to see that he was looking for news. One subject came up continually in his conversation: the immense possibilities offered by the nature of the surrounding country for parachutage. He was sure that we had already received one and that others were to come, etc. Even Allied soldiers could easily come down round about the camp and then what magnificent work could be done. It was really too obvious that he was looking for news but he did not succeed very well because I agreed with him on every point and even made things worse than they were and seemed to be. Our possibilities in men, munitions, etc, were very great. Parachutages had already arrived and more were expected. We were even expecting very soon an immense landing of airborne Allied troops. He had been looking for details: now he had them. If he was really a "résistance" member he would soon learn the truth. If, as we suspected, he was a spy and, once more, if he managed to escape from the camp the news he would bring might discourage a too sudden attack. I felt firmly convinced that he was a spy and finding an excuse for leaving him I made my way cautiously to where I knew I would find the lieutenant and, after explaining my reasons for suspecting the newcomer, asked him to arrest and question him.

While we speaking in a small clump of trees which separated HQ and another section of the camp we heard the arrival of trucks and hearty cheers. On coming out of our shelter the lieutenant went straight out into the open while I took an indirect route and came out from behind one of the old farm's outhouses, we saw the reason for the disturbance.

Two of the camp's private cars were filled with our men and carrying more arms than usual, They had also brought in two trucks full of unshaven and white-faced, tired-looking men whose smiles breathed deliverance. But the finest sight of all was that of a French militia officer in full uniform (minus his kepi which was worn at a jaunty angle by his guard) handcuffed and looking not at all pleased with himself. One of the commandos had raided early that morning a prison at the M.d'O where Jews and aliens had been incarcerated on the sole charge of their nationality or religion. The operation had been short but very effective. Several of the militia guards had been killed, others had fled but none of our men had been wounded and they had succeeded not only in liberating the prisoners but also in capturing the prison chief who was notorious for his cruelty to the prisoners. Some of our men were for killing him immediately but the camp commander intervened and insisted on a fair trial. While we were attending to the liberated prisoners whose first needs seemed to be a good meal, a thorough toilet and a change of underclothing, our prisoner was locked up in a pig-sty. The prisoners were witness of his cruelty and he was condemned to death. Half an hour later, after preparing his own grave, he was shot at short range by one of our men whose father had been killed by the militia. But he must have been "persuaded" to talk before his death (when going into the big field below the camp with his spade I noticed heavy wheals on his face and neck) because soon after his execution two rapid cars of men heavily armed set out for an unknown destination. During their absence I reminded out lieutenant of the suspected newcomer but he told me not to worry any more about him, that he had given orders. A few hours later the cars came back but instead of two, there were three. The expedition had been fruitful because they had brought with them ten prisoners; nine men and a woman. Immediately on their arrival two were sorted out; one man of about thirty-four to thirty-six years of age with only one arm and the woman, his "maîtresse". Their trial was rapidly effectuated. The vowed that it was he who had disclosed to the militia the date and nature of the convoy which had been decimated a day or so before and from which we had received the young man with the fractured knee. He could not deny it because the militia officer who had been executed that morning had disclosed his name as well as those of the other prisoners. But seeing himself discovered not only did he avow his crime but he also admitted his responsibility for several others. The woman would not speak but kept a very stubborn silence. Both of them were condemned to death but the woman could save her life if she would speak. Both were led down to the same big field which had seen the morning's execution. As the man was disabled he was a sad sight because on his way from the military tribunal to the field almost everyone had struck him, the young men dug his grave but the woman had to help. When everything was ready he was made to stand with his back to the firing squad which was made up chiefly of survivors of his treachery and in a few seconds all was over. The woman was invited to take his place on the edge of the grave (they were placed so as to fall into the hole and give less trouble). She cried but seemed brave enough. She was made to face the rifles but after the first order she fell on her knees sobbing and calling out "I shall talk." On a word from the officer she was led alone up the field back to the low-roofed room where a short time before she stood for judgement side by side with her "amant". Still sobbing, a nervous wreck who had lost all her pride, she gave a list of facts, names and addresses which was carefully reserved for further use. That evening I was sent for by the lieutenant to learn some very bad news: Our "suspect" was nowhere t be found; he had completely disappeared. Had our double capture and its possible consequences frightened him? In any case he was off and it was really dangerous.

But a more embarrassing dilemma presented itself. The camp's population was increasing too rapidly. We were five thousand and for the greater part entirely inexperienced in any kind of warfare. There was not enough arms or munitions to afford even a small cover to this multitude because the parachutage was not forthcoming. Feed reserves were dwindling rapidly. It was impossible to carry on. There was only one thing to do: dismiss the camp and keep only a few who had been there since the beginning. What a cold shower for all those who had left work and home to take to the "maquis". And how were they going to go back home? The roads were continually controlled by Germans and militia and towns and villages were full of informers. What was going to happen to all these men? These thoughts raced through my mind all evening and all night.

Next morning, shortly after breakfast, the news was given simultaneously in every sector. At HQ it was like a bomb. Many showed disgust at the lack or organisation. Others blamed Britain for not sending supplies. In brief the news disappointed everyone. The dismissal began; company after company came to the headquarters and after a few words from their officers disposed arms and munitions at their feet prior to their preparing themselves for a long trek home because the camp commander had forbidden everyone to use the camp's vehicles. Everyone was downcast. Those who were leaving parted in small groups with trailing footsteps. It was a scene of perfect desolation. I was determined on one thing and that was that I should not be chased away. I was there and if I had come so far it was not without effort so I was going to stay. I was musing this when all of a sudden one of our small cars came rocking down the old country road at breakneck speed. "Everyone to arms!" cried one of the junior officers seated on the right front mudguard. "The Germans are coming." Some rushed for the wood behind the farm which housed HQ but others remained quite calm awaiting orders. The arms and munitions which had been left but the companies already disarmed and dismissed were divided out. The lieutenant commanding HQ took a company of which I was and gave instructions to two other officers to take each one another company and make their way to a great wood ten kilométres away. We were all to go by a different route and there await forthcoming instructions. It was of no avail to try and make a stand because we were too much inferior in arms, munitions and experience against a heavy armoured, experienced column. The other two companies left ahead of us. We unlocked the nine prisoners from their pig-sty and, keeping them in the middle of us, we began our long march through the woods. Our double column advanced with every care. Most of the time we were in the wood but twice we had to cross a wide-open space. Each time before leaving cover the lieutenant's field glasses assured us against enemy presence. At last without incident except for a few false alarms caused by the movement of certain other companies towards the same wood, we arrived safely at our destination which was an immense pinewood covering the slopes and summit of a steep hill. The position reminded me very much of the first camp I had left at G.-. Here with plenty of arms, munitions and food a few hundred men could have held for a long time because there was only one second-class road and it was at the foot of the hill. With reliable men in such a position nothing could have passed. The place seemed to me almost invulnerable. Only heavy artillery and aviation could have dislodged a fighting unit from it and all around was undercover as eventual retreat was not a great problem. However we sheltered down in a small sheltered clearing about halfway up the hill and after leaving reliable sentries at the important points the lieutenant held a council of war. We were in a good position but were in great need of food. Very few had eaten much during the day and, as "an enemy fights on its stomach" something had to be done about it, In any case we had to wait until dusk because we had no idea of the situation around us. We still had our prisoners with us and they were an extra worry. Time dragged on until dusk and then the lieutenant asked for volunteers to go back across country to the HQ to bring back some food. Ten of us stepped out and duly armed, the officer at our head, we attacked inversely the road we had taken to come here early in the afternoon. It was dusk in the open but under cover of the woods it was very dark. As all orts of rumours had been going around we had to be very cautious. Walking in two single files, one on each side of the car tracks under the leafy arches, we kept our eyes and ears open. Not a word was spoken, no one dared light a cigarette and in the open we wriggled our way across the fields. Every sound made us look up until at last we arrived within three-quarters of a mile of the cam. Here we spread out fanwise and every muscle and nerve ready for action we made our way to the farmhouse. Sounds of voices came to us but on listening attentively we understood that it was French that was being spoken and decidedly not German. To make sure of the nature of its occupants we made our way to the small windows and, Oh surprise, we saw some of our friends packing up butter, cheese and sugar prior to taking them to their respective companies farther away in the woods. When we interrupted we were almost fired upon. However "all is well that ends well". The Germans had been coming directly towards our camp but had passed on to another of the same type but much better armed some thirty kilométres or so farther up in the hills. The news was bad enough but it gave us time to breathe and to organise ourselves a little. It seemed to me that much would depend on the result of this engagement. In the meantime we had immediate needs to satisfy. At HQ there was a considerable store of butter, cheese, jam, sugar and two big barrels of rich, red wine. We therefore set to, to have a good meal and half an hour later felt decidedly better.

During our night march I had noticed a very tall young man, rather well dressed and, a striking feature in the maquis, who wore a soft hat of a very clear and striking colour. It was curiosity about his so tidy dress etc. but also his frank and amicable smile which attracted me towards him. He looked very intelligent and well educated. Such a companion would have been a perfect blessing for me because I had made no friends and in my lonely situation would have been delighted to be able to speak with someone about anything else but the worn current topics which were everyday conversation at the camp where the educational standard was not high. During our rough and ready meal we spoke quite a lot together and from that evening onward there grew a friendship which was to strengthen day by day in the midst of common risks.

Physically restored and rested we filled sacks with every useful foodstuffs we could put our hands on and carry without too much hindrance. Heavily laden but feeling more at ease we struck out in the direction of the retreat marching as rapidly as possible and thinking of our companions cold and hungry in the evening dampness of the wood (we were at an altitude of 1000 metres above sea level and in spite of the season the evenings were very cold). We were going along at a good speed in the open and nearing a little hamlet when all of a sudden a voice rang out in the darkness and summoned us to stop. We obeyed immediately. "One of the covering companies has come forward to make an outpost in the old abandoned farmhouse on the outskirts of the little village," said the lieutenant. "Let's advance to make ourselves known." We went forward a few paces and the officer made himself known. The sentry then asked for the password. "Belfast," announced the lieutenant but the sentry seemed not well satisfied. He seemed particularly nervous and toyed too much with his Tommy-gun for our liking. We were at a loss and wondered why the day's events had disturbed everything and, as we learned later, a new password had been announced by an estafette[2] who had gone round the companies in our absence. The officer moved forward a little trying to explain who he was, insisting on the fact that the young man must know him. The latter agreed that he recognised the lieutenant but that there was only one thing that mattered and that was the password. On witnessing such stupid stubbornness we began to lose patience. The young man seemed very nervous and above all very much frightened. At any moment his arm might go off in his hands and perhaps cause some very regrettable damage. On a careful sign from the lieutenant and after an understanding glance at one another we all put our arms at the ready. The lieutenant them made a stealthy sign and we closed in quietly while he explained to the sentry how stupid he was and that if we had been enemies he would have been dead a few minutes before because we were all armed. In a second he was disarmed and sat down like a man who had just furnished a great

---

[2] *dispatch rider*

effort. He was dying of fear and his nerves had been the better of him. We brought him to the company's headquarters where he was sent to rest a little and where we learned the new password. But we could not stay very long, of comrades must be fed so off we went again into the night. After an uneventful journey troubled only by cattle in the fields and above all behind the hedges who decided to move about just when we arrived. Once the camp was reached and the food divided out we lay down for a well-earned rest. I managed to sleep until 2.00 a.m. but I had then to rise and walk about in order to chase the benumbing wet cold. The prisoners were all huddled together in the middle of a mile of slumbering men. They had not tried to escape but had they been found wandering in the woods by German soldiers their sort might have been very much like ours: a bullet first, questions afterwards if it was still possible.

At sunrise we moved off again in the direction of the camp where the unfortunate sentry had given us so much worry the night before to find that HQ had been established in the little village. News was not good. The M… camp had been very severely attacked. The "maquis" had been obliged retreat but the result of the first engagement had been decidedly in their favour. German reinforcements had moved up to help and the camp could expect to be in for a hard time. The latest bulletin announced that a heavy onslaught had already begun, even the German aviation was taking part in it. There was only one solution: rear-guard action as far as possible. One thing was certain: our turn would be coming next and we were in no way able to withstand such an attack. The remaining companies must be dismissed or, if not, taken by their officers to another part of the region where in co-operation with the regional command they were to take up guerrilla activity to the best of their ability. The lieutenant in charge of HQ invited me to join him and leave for another county which was very advantageous for guerrillas. However, I refrained because my friend whose conduct had struck me during our nightly march had spoken to me of a small independent but very active organisation whose headquarters was only forty miles away. According to his description of this new unit (new for me but not new with regard to activity, the chief had been one of the first in the region to receive portable emitting and receiving wireless sets by parachutage from London). The unit took the form of a light and rapid column whose chief function was the maintenance of law and order in the region and liaison between the different camps and more considerable sections of "maquisards". I very naturally preferred following my friend than going away to a more or less problematic destiny with the lieutenant, I could certainly have made a considerable blunder but since I have realised that I chose the better part.

Together Bob and I made our preparations. Our luggage was not very considerable. I had a small haversack and an attaché case in which were all my belongings. My friend had a rucksack. In the exodus of the night before we had managed to procure several objects because everything had been left topsy-turvy. We kept two leather jackets (which were later to be very useful) a sack containing about three hundred rounds of Sten-gun ammunition and, what was more useful and precious, about fifteen pounds of sugar. We loaded ourselves with this last article because of its security and resulting trading power among the peasants. We were setting out on a forty-mile trek without any food whatsoever as we had to be practical. Our "preparatifs" ended we set out without a map or even a compass knowing that it was impossible to use the roads and that the Germans were in force thirty miles away. Our strength was in our quickly made friendship and our confidence in the future. The county we were heading for was very mountainous. From where we started, the heights were very visible and among them on "puy" the highest in the range, served as a landmark because our destination was very near it. We set out at about nine o'clock in the morning. The sun was blazing overhead and we were in high spirits. Keeping to the fields and having a watchful eye all around us we walked on with a long stride (my short training in the Foreign Legion stood me in good stead). After a very short time the countryside became flat and bare. Cover was scarce as we had to redouble precautions. Across field after field, jumping barbed-wire fences we went our ears and eyes continually open for the sound or sight of vehicular traffic.

About an hour after our departure we were marching gaily across a wide stretch of fields when the sound of motor traffic struck our ears. Instinctively we fell flat and were pleased to have done so because a minute or two later a full enemy column of about thirty vehicles passed on the road about two hundred yards away. The alarm past we set off again but our jaunty pace was not to last very long. Ten minutes later the staccato bark of automatic gunfire filled the air. We were in a hollow as we attacked the slope on our hands and knees as quickly but cautiously as possible. On arriving at the crest of the hill we saw what we had feared had happened: a small section (two trucks) either from our camp which had been disbanded or from the other big camp farther up had fallen on the enemy column. In the impossibility of either turning back or breaking through they had accepted a hopeless combat. The fight was going on about three hundred yards away and from our position we could see quite clearly what was happening. Our comrades, who seemed few in number, seeing the impossibility of attempting to resist had begun a fighting retreat. Their courage was magnificent but they had undertaken a hopeless task. The surrounding country afforded absolutely no cover and thus gave the enemy every facility of spotting and picking them out as they moved. But the "maquisards" seemed determined to fight for it. They seemed to be practising a cover tactic: two Bren-guns constituted the only heavy arms of the section, one remained in position spraying the enemy column in as wide a range as possible while the other moved uphill firing now and then and taking position to cover the retreat of its fellow. There seemed to be about twenty-five or thirty men of the "maquis" but already three or four dotted the greensward. The goal of their retreat seemed to be a small cattle shelter situated on the green slope at about five hundred yards from the road. Unhappily few were to reach it. The Germans had advanced two armoured cars and from this shelter two heavy machine-guns and two small cannons made ravage among the little band of warriors. The poor chaps fell one after another. Two Bren-gun assistants went down at the same time. Immediately two or three of those who had been retreating with it closed in and seeing their friends falling fast seemed to decide that they must reach the little shelter as quickly as possible, broke into a run carrying ammunition, charged and the gun itself. Their comrades followed their example and in a burst of speed made for the little corrugated iron construction. Only about eight of them arrived at their goal and one of the Brens remained on the field in the arms of one who had done his best to bring it home. But such a shelter was of no avail. The two armoured cars passed through the hedge and followed by infantry climbed relentlessly the green slope. Our men fired bravely and with desperate courage from the space between the roof and the top of the walls which were only about five feet high but their end had come. A few small shells joined to a constant stream of machine-gun fire soon reduced their effort to nothing. In a few minutes all was over. The improvised fort was reduced to silence. We thought it was the end but unhappily it was not. A section of infantry surrounded the place which a few seconds later rocked under the impetus of three loud detonations. The savages, wishing to be sure of their kill, had thrown grenades into the place. What we witness next can only be forgotten by the souvenir[3] of greater atrocities seen later. The brutes went into what was left of the shelter and shortly after emerged trailing on the ground two unfortunate forms which they seem to gratify with the worse of rough treatments. What seemed to be an officer came forward and stooping over the forms seemed with fierce gesticulations to speak to them. He seemed to be very angry and lifting his foot gave them kick after kick. One of the bystanders, afraid I suppose that the officer might tire himself, helped him in this very courageous work. Each time the officer rose again after stooping over these poor forms the brutal treatment began again. At last he made a sign and we heard two Tommy-gun salvos. Our unfortunate comrades' sufferings were over. Then some of the soldiers went into the ruins, others spread themselves out over the field and from the shots we learned that all their young lives were away together. We breathed a silent prayer for them all seeing their end a

---

[3] *memory*

probable ending of our own adventure. The enemy gathered up their belongings, among which three wounded and one dead, very seriously hit and after setting fire to the hay and straw in the shelter and destroying the two trucks which must have been damaged during the engagement by putting grenades or bombs in their engines they resumed their interrupted journey. Bob and I waited until the column was underway and out of sight muttering the while what we thought of these savages and then we made our way towards the battlefield. As we approached, heads bare, we had further proofs of the enemy's ruthless brutality. Every man who had fallen was turned over on his back but few were recognisable. The automatic arms had been satanically used to smash the "marquisards"' faces. When we approached near the ruined and still smouldering shelter we found the two who probably had been questioned and had refused to reply. Their faces, like the others were in a pitiful state but not less than that of the state of their bodies. They seemed to have been literally torn in pieces. When dragged out they must have had a very short time to live. How our blood boiled at the thought of the treatment they had received! Could the barbarians not have allowed them to die in peace? I will not give any details of the state of the mangled bodies in the smoking shelter. They were really too gruesome. An inspection of the other victims the same terrible detail: disfiguration. The enemy had not even thought of or even found burial for their victims so we decided to try and find the nearest village and after seeing someone responsible arrange for a respectable resting-place for our young comrades.

After searching the horizon we saw the outline of a little hamlet not so far off. In half an hour we arrived at it and, after making sure of the absence of the enemy we found the mayor who greeted us wholeheartedly and after offering a substantial refreshment to which we really could not do justice in the circumstances asked us to guide him and a few of the villagers with bullocks and carts to the miniature battlefield. In spite of the danger of a new enemy invasion the bodies were gathered with all due respect and covered with what poor flowers the peasants could gather affectionately laid in a row in the hall of the village "mairie". When we left the village our hearts were heavy but we were more than ever determined to do our utmost to avenge our unfortunate comrades. The road seemed to us long and dreary. The sad spectacle we had witnessed had cooled the joy of our departure from the camp. Grimly we plodded on. During the first part of our forced march across the uneven and often very thickly wooded country conversation lagged. We were both plunged in thought. But soon we realised the mutual unfairness of our silence. The going was heavy. We could not think of following the regular roads first of all for our own safety and secondly we wished to march as the crow flies in order to arrive more quickly and, if possible, before nightfall. More than once the passages of enemy columns on the roads obliged us to crawl like snakes across fields. The strain was beginning to tell on us. We had had little or no sleep the night before and had marched more than thirty-five kilométres. The slight refreshment we had been able to take at our unfortunate comrades' mortuary village seemed far away. Hunger and fatigue began to tell on us and we felt the need for a rest and some food. It was then I realised how good had been Bob's idea of bringing the sugar. We stopped in a small hamlet on the slope of a very wooded hill and after hiding our arms and munitions we went into the first house offering two pounds of sugar for some bread, cheese and wine. The reception was quite cold. Gruffly we were told to sit on a bench outside in the blazing sun. We tried to stay there but soon changed our place to behind the house. As soon as we had moved the farmer came out and angrily asked us why we were moving about and what we were wishing to see. I felt that he looked upon us as suspicious characters and decided risk the password in quite a roundabout way so as not to have it known by an enemy. "Do you know Metz? Have you been in it?" I asked the farmer. He looked at me in a quiet way for a few seconds then in a casual way replied, "Yes, it is on the line." I smiled, then he cried "Why in the name of everything did you not speak before. Come in quickly. The country is full of German and militia spies." When he led us into the house with a smile on his face his wife, rather pale, looked at him questioningly. "We have almost thrown two of our boys out, Marie Thérèse. Quick, get them something good to eat while I go down to the cave to bring up some of the best. Tell Jean-Louis and Martin to come out of the room and that everything is all right." Like magic beautiful white country bread with cold chicken, pork, home-made sausage (a speciality of the hills) appeared on the table. A few minutes later two stalwart youths of about sixteen and eighteen years of age, both in maquis uniforms, appeared from a doorway at the bottom of the kitchen and with boyish grins came forward to shake hands. We were soon conversing like old friends. The farmer arrived with two big jugs of wine and an old dusty bottle in each pocket. As soon as we had begun eating and drinking our host explained his attitude. During the last few days several villages had been visited by German or militia squads accompanied by civilians. His two sons had been in the maquis. Their sector had been heavily attacked the day before at dawn and after fighting for about twenty-four hours the enemy, thanks to his numerical and armoured superiority, had gained the advantage. The men had been ordered to disperse and keep themselves in contact with their local "résistance" chief, who in the present case was the farmer himself, with a view to later action. They had seen us coming and stopping in the woods to hide our arms and munitions in the tree forks before entering into the village. Our dress and, above all, our too cultured way of speaking denoted strangers to the district and did not make us look like maquisards. On their father's orders the two sons had taken position duly armed in the back room ready to shoot us down if we had tried to enter the apartment. When we had tried to go round to the back of the house the farmer had himself slipped a gun into his pocket before coming to see what we were about. He assured us that we were very near death. We all laughed heartily about it and during the conversation I told them that I was British. How pleased they were. The farmer immediately went back to the cellar and came back with a bottle of fine old cognac to celebrate the presence under his roof of the first British subject he had ever met. I shall never forget how happy these people were. For a short time we all forgot our worries and the perils of the moment. However we were obliged to think of our goal and in spite of repeated invitations to stay with them a day or so until the district quietened down we took to the road again but not before leaving the major part of our sugar supply to thank these so kind peasants whose simple hospitality had done so much to cheer us up.

The road became more and more difficult because of the mountains. Following our plans we kept to the woods, fields and pathways avoiding the main roads and keeping a sharp eye and ear. The "puy" became nearer and nearer and Bob began to recognise the countryside. Now and then we stopped at an auberge to drink a glass of wine and usually enquired if any of the occupation troops had been seen lately. Almost everyone spoke of their regular passing in the district so I was quite pleased when on arriving at the foot of a very steep and thickly wooded hill Bob triumphantly announced that the small town we were heading for was at the summit. We attacked the slope with all our remaining vigour and were soon near the top. With the town in sight we redoubled attention because it was on a very important and strategical road often used by the Germans. As we had to be sure of the presence or absence of enemy troops we decided to await a passer-by in order to know what was going on. Soon a middle-aged woman came in direction of the locality as Bon stepped out from under cover to ask whether or not there was enemy presence. The woman replied in the negative and offered to go on a few yards ahead of us and put down her errand basket if she noticed anything unusual. We thanked her wholeheartedly and soon were sitting in a café where Bob was very well known awaiting the arrival of our new chief.

During our long trek my companion and I had had time to get to know one another quite well. I had told Bob who I was, how I had happened to be in the "résistance" and in what way I had come to the "maquis". In turn he had told me who he was and what he had done in the movement. In 1940 he had been a student in higher mathematics ready to go to university. His goal had been the military career like his father who was a general in the French army. His mother was of one of the very old French families and his grandparents on his mother's side were a count and countess. After the French armistice he had gone to the Alps with the résistance movement and had worked there a certain time. From there he had been sent to Switzerland where he had been interned in an aliens' work camp. After about nine months internment he had, thanks to some influential person, been able to regain his country where he continued his activity to end up where I had found him in the big camp. The reward for his work had not been very great. He had spent money, a lot more than he had earned. His father had been deported by the Germans in 1942. His mother had been taken prisoner but after a month's informal life had been released. As he said, the family home had been broken up. The enemy had ransacked their home. His mother, youngest brother and two sisters were living in one place while his other brother, about two years his junior, was hiding in the country. Bob's situation would have been better but, like myself, he had refused to become officially affiliated to any particular branch of the "résistance" because of the dividing political tendencies which differentiated them and which I was so much to regret later when I had the chance to see their terrible consequences for the country and the common cause.

After waiting for about an hour (the sun had gone down and night was creeping in) we were disturbed by the sound of the arrival of motor cars which stopped a few yards from the café. After telling us not to move the proprietor went to the door only to come straight back to announce the arrival of our new chief. We went out to see three dark coloured cars each flying above the radiator the "résistance" pennant: French tricolour and Lorraine cross in the middle of the white strip. Each car had a crew of four men. All were dressed in black blouses and ski trousers of the same colour. There wore black cloth berets with skull and cross-bone sign of the commandos. Among them Bob pointed out a quite small and dapper man and announced him as G… We went forward and Bob, who knew him well, made the necessary presentations. To justify my identity I showed him my passport. He was very kind but I could not help noticing in his determined and courageous face something which I was only able to define later. I was quite surprised when he calmly announced that he did not wish to take us to his HQ in the mountain but he said that he would care for us and after ordering a good meal and paying for a room in the locality's only hotel bid us goodnight warning us to be ready very early next morning when he would come to take us. However we were very grateful to him and we had the refreshing sensation of having a good wash, undressing and snuggling down between fresh, clean sheets for a well-earned night's rest.

Next morning at 7.00 a.m. one of the black cars of the night before called for us and we were soon on the way to a new destination. After a few unexplained stops here and there we arrived in a quite considerable little town. We stopped in the square and after a short time another of the cars joined us out of which stepped the chief. Very politely he asked us how we felt, etc. and losing no time invited us into a quiet corner in a nearby café. I noticed that the newcomers addressed our chief as "Captain" and that he called the younger and more intelligent-looking of the two "Lieutenant". In his very brief and military manner G…, whom we were always to know as the "Chief" explained the situation. The town was to become a secondary "résistance" HQ for the county. There were many reasons for this choice but mainly its position as a sort of crossroads between four very important towns which were frequently employed by the enemy as meeting places before a raid in one or other direction. Two important railway lines passed not very far away. As it was not very big the Germans had never stayed in it very long so news could be centralised and plans drawn up more easily and less dangerously than in many of the other towns. But it was indispensable to see to the security of the inhabitants and for that reason the town had to be "covered", that is to say warned in case of a probable enemy visit so that nothing convicting could be found which might cause reprisals which, we had experience of it, could be really terrible. Until now the "covering" had only been realised on one side. There were still three important roads to be watched. The "Chief" had spotted a sight for the "look-out" and suggested that Bob and I should take upon us the task of founding the post. He warned us that nothing had been prepared and that the little village which was to be our home while we were fulfilling this mission had never been sounded as to its patriotic sentiments. My companion was presented as "Bob" while I was only "Maurice". Not a word was said about my real nationality, I was simply a Frenchman like the others. The "Chief" seemed to have all the authority; he did all the talking while the others listened. After receiving our consent for the undertaking he left some money with the "Captain" and after telling us that he would be back before mid-day with twenty-four hours rations told us to enjoy ourselves at his expense, to have a walk around the town but to be in the square near eleven o'clock at the latest. We obeyed him and at exactly eleven he was there with another gentleman who, I learned later, was photographer in the town. We were given each one our rations but after leaving the heavier part of our baggage behind us prepared to go off. The "Chief brought us to a hôtel near the railway station where our new comrade awaited us with a highly powered 500cc Indian motorcycle. We were told to examine the situation in the village, see the possibilities of accomplishing our task and to await the "Chief's" visit. The weight of three passengers did not seem to hinder the vehicle's speed. We left the town, Bob sitting on the pillion cushion and me occupying the small space between the same cushion and the diver's saddle. Everything went well; the road was in a quite good condition and the motorcycle attacked the numerous hills without a falter. As our driver had explained to us, the road had only one inconvenience: it ran through an undulating but very bare countryside. A sudden encounter with a German unit meant certain death. The twenty-five-kilométre run was accomplished uneventfully and very soon our driver stopped announcing the terminus.

We were at the junction of two roads. The main road continued towards C…, very important as it led to one of the biggest railway centres in the centre of

Francc, was a German and militia stronghold. The road which met it led to the martyr town which is now famed for having been the deathbed of Kessler, chief of the Gestapo for the southern region of France. Further ahead lay the most important town of the county, another German and militia nest. About two hundred and fifty yards back down the way we had come was another very important road coming from the same central town but by way of the highest mountain in the region. Such was the situation. Our work was to guard the town we had left against any sudden enemy incursion from any of these directions. Everything was to be organised so we had to begin as soon as possible. A few yards from our arriving point stood a small village comprising eight houses and a half-demolished cowshed. All the building except one straggled along the sides of the road on our right. The other farmhouse stood on the left of the main road not far from the junction. Now that we had sized up the situation it was necessary to find somewhere to make our quarters. We could not think of putting up in any peasant's home because if ever we were discovered it would mean the burning of the house and the shooting or deportation of the family. But we had not long to wait. The arrival of the motorcycle had not passed unnoticed in the village. Soon a middle-aged peasant came down the road from the village and as we saluted him he stopped. He said that he supposed we were from the "maquis". On our enquiry as to the reason for his supposition he said that having seen a "résistance car (which we now recognised as being that of the "Chief") sopped in the village a few days previously and its occupants examining the village and the roads he supposed that there had been questions of something and very simply he offered to help in any way he could. We were not very keen on telling him our business but simply said that we were going to stay a few days in the neighbourhood. We assured him that our presence was not going to endanger the village in any way because we did not wish to stay in it. In a few words he explained the if he could be of any assistance we were not to hesitate to call upon him and showed us his home, the second last on the left. Before leaving us he spoke of the village as being very quiet and void of pro-Nazi feelings. We would find friends there on condition that we did nothing to disturb their quiet rural life. When he had left us we began to scout around. The half-demolished cowshed seemed quite a good place to bivouac. It was vertical to the road and the half which pointed towards the wood was intact while the other part was in ruins. The entrance was from the ruined side and in the good part was a small loft just long enough to hold two men. As it had been used to keep straw the thatch was in a good state so in spite of the draughts we would at least be dry. There was still a little straw in the loft so we could at least make a bed. To be on the peasants' good side we resolved to get to know the owner of the ruin and went to see the farmer who had offered his help. He informed us that he was the owner, gave us the permission to use it and even promised to give us some more fresh straw for which we were very thankful. He informed that there was another village about a mile and a half away by the main road which could be reached in about five minutes through the fields. There was a telephone there. With all these details we began to know how to act and made our plans accordingly. From our improvised HQ we commanded a view of one of these roads. The great difficulty was the distance between the post and the telephone so we arranged that while one could stay in the loft to take a rest the other, protected by a thin belt of trees, would take the look-out on the other side of the road ready to race for the telephone. This stratagem was rendered necessary by the fact that if we had both stayed in the post we could not have passed across the road to go to the telephone until the column had completely passed and as the town was only thirty-five kilométres away and certain columns very long the warning would come too late to be effective. Having thus made our we proceeded to the little town. Our relations with the peasants were very evident. One of them especially, the mother of two sons who had her husband a prisoner in Germany, was very good to us. She invited us to dinner and refused any money. Bob and I decided to take a three-hour vigil each night. During that day and the following night nothing happened. Next morning the "Chief" arrived suddenly. When we explained the situation he seemed quite pleased with our organisation and promised to be back next day with a field telephone and an electrician. In the interval we were to look for a suitable place for it. We soon found the place: the last house on the left was unoccupied. It was at a bend in the road and screened by a few high trees. As nobody had occupied it for quite a time the garden which separated it from the road was overrun with weeds. The telephone wires passed on its side of the road. It would thus be simple to "tap" the line, pass the wire through the trees and under cover of the luxuriant growth of weeds bring it to the house. The woman whose husband was a prisoner had the key and willingly lent it to us. Next morning the telephone was put in and we felt a little more at ease. There was only one danger, that of an enemy column stopping in thc village and finding the apparatus. We would have to deal abruptly with such an event because the village security had to pass before anything else.

The next two or three days and nights went by quite quietly. We were constantly in contact with the "Chief". News was very good. On 18th June the group had arrested Kessler's "maîtresse" as well as her father and brother who arrived from France's famed thermal stations on the next day. We had heard this in the morning and felt very happy about it when at the beginning of the afternoon a quite considerable German column through the village in the direction of the town. We immediately rang up but the operator did not seem to be at her post. The post office had put us through to the "résistance" telephone but nobody seemed to be there and a precious minute or two was lost. However we gave the message to the post office and asked it to be sent around the town as quickly as possible. The delay this caused was the reason for the loss of the three important prisoners mentioned above. As the news came too late the prisoners were hurried out of the prison and these three managed to separate themselves from the others in a wood and join the enemy column before it left the town.

Late that evening the "Chief" arrived to pay a surprise visit. With him were twelve men and we were to go with the group on a special mission. While we were racing through the night "Chief" explained the situation. Having learned that the Germans were preparing a "clear-out" in the county he had wanted to be sure of their position and to this end had sent out three men of the local "résistance", two gendarmes and a civilian with a motorcycle and side-car giving them instructions not to go further than a certain locality and to telephone from there. They had left very shortly after the enemy column's departure in the opposite direction but had given no sign of life. We were to go and see what had happened. We had two fast motor cars and were led by the even faster motorcycle and the driver who had brought Bob and I to our new post. If the enemy had camped in any of the smaller villages we were to try to free our friends if they were prisoners. The cars were like little arsenals so in the night we had little to be afraid of. After a wild course we stopped at the outskirts of a big village. All lights extinguished we left the vehicles on the side of the road with three men, the drivers, ready to put the engines in motion in case of emergency. By groups of three we examined the village which was in complete darkness. We found traces neither of a column's passage not of a combat. The village was strangely quiet. Not a light. Before going any further we needed to have some details as to the afternoon's happenings. Did our men pass here? Were there any Germans in the village since morning? The Chief decided to interrogate one of the farmers. We approached one of the biggest houses and knocked loudly on the door. In spite of repeated knockings no one answered. We then decided to employ a new stratagem. One of our men spoke German fluently. In a loud voice he summoned the peasant to come down and open the door. I did not understand the whole of his soliloquy I remarked the repetition of the well-known word "Achtung." The effect was instantaneous. A light shone in one of the upstairs windows and in a very short time a dishevelled farmer opened the door. We immediately pushed him aside and entered the house. He seemed very astonished on seeing the nature of the intruders. The surprise passed he began to ask us, as only French people can do, in a colourful language what were we looking for and what was our reason for awakening him in the middle of the night. After waiting until the "steam had blown off" the "Chief" in his usual quiet way asked him why our repeated knocking could not rouse him while a few words in German opened his eyes and his house like a "sesame". He immediately retorted that the peasants had enough of seeing farms and villages burned and that, for them, the Germans were to be obeyed without murmur not by love but by fear. On being asked if he had seen our comrades he replied stubbornly that he had been in the fields all day and had noticed nothing. But there was something about his way which led us to think the contrary. The "Chief" asked him to gather his wits together and to think but the farmer replied to his injunction by a fit of ill-temper in which he told us to go everywhere. We tried to persuade him how important it was for us to know something of the whereabouts of our companions, how their very lives depended upon us, he only continued to vociferate and tell us how much we were putting the peasants' goods and homes in danger by out persistent acts of sabotage and our attacks upon the German columns. We saw that it was impossible to learn anything from him in this way so the "Chief" decided to take more important measures. He threatened to set the barn on fire if the farmer did not say what he knew. We felt that we had discovered the soft spot. On an order we each took a grenade from our belt and carrying them ostentatiously we made our way to the barn which was just above the stables behind the house. Escorted by the "Chief" the farmer accompanied us. He was trembling in every limb and strangely silent. His silence was only broken when we opened the barn doors and by the light of a flash lamp chose each one where to throw his missile. "I will tell you," cried the unhappy man. "Your men stopped in the village this afternoon. They asked if we knew the whereabouts of the German column which was in the district. We knew by those who had been to the big town to buy their provisions that the enemy was camping near the next village. Being afraid that the Germans might come into the village while the "maquis" was there and that our homes and livestock might suffer from it we told the three men that we knew nothing of there the enemy was but that perhaps the inhabitants of the next village could enlighten them. A short time after their departure we heard the sound of a very brief combat. We have seen neither "maquis" nor Germans since." The story was briefly told. We were too disgusted to reply. This was only a repetition of what had often happened in the annals of the "maquis". Through fear of reprisals many had sent courageous young men to death in front of an enemy sometimes a hundred to one superior in numbers. As much as possible the "maquis" never attacked near or in villages but sometimes a hot-headed young officer would make a blunder or a small supplies convoy would be surprised and obliged to fight and the result was very often disastrous for the nearest village or small town. On quite a number of occasions the enemy, especially the SS, did not even await such a provocation to sow blood and fire on their way. However we had not a great deal of time for these considerations.

Leaving the farmer where he was in front of the barn he had preferred to courageous men's lives we hurried back to the cars. Our friends might be prisoners or even lying wounded on the road. We must do all within our power to ascertain their fate. Leaving the guilty village behind us we travelled on cautiously, all lights out, trusting to our eyes to discern any obstacle or enemy we anon came near the next village. About a mile from the habitations we stopped the cars and, after hiding them in a small thicket, we continued in Indian file our Tommy-guns at the ready. Soon the first houses loomed up in the darkness. We left the road and approached the village in a half-inch with the orders to meet one another on the square if all went well. Our "marche d'approche" proved uneventful. Together again we picked out the village mayor's house and knocked at the door. In a few seconds a light went on and a man's voice from the window enquired as to our mission. Invited to come down the mayor soon opened the door and invited us in. Recognising our uniform and armbands he came to the point at once. Two of our men had been instantaneously killed. The third had been found with his two legs broken a short distance away. The injured man was in the mayor's brother's house (his own was too apt to be visited) while the bodies were in the village hall. We were immediately brought to see them. They had not been mutilated in any way but their bodies were riddled with machine-gun bullets. After saluting them and receiving from the mayor the assurance that they would have an honourable burial we went to see our wounded friend. He was propped up in a comfortable bed a little pale but looking nevertheless none the worse for his experience. The local doctor had made temporary dressings for his broken limbs and the patient seemed surprisingly at ease. In a few words he explained the unhappy end of their scouting expedition. They had stopped at the other village as ordered. There they could have no news so they decided to push forward. About a mile from the village at a bend in the road they met unexpectedly the German column. The companion in the sidecar immediately opened fire with his Bren-gun, killed an officer who was standing up in the first armoured car and wounded a soldier near him. In reply the enemy opened fire with machine and Bren-guns. The driver of the motorcycle and the man in the sidecar died immediately. He fell from the pillion seat, rolled over into a field and ran towards a small bridge which spanned a rather deep gully. The enemy kept firing at him so he fell from the bridge shamming death and broke his two legs in falling. He lay in this position until he was gathered up by a peasant who had heard him moaning. It was impossible for us to take him with us as we returned as quickly as possible to the town, sought a surgeon and in a very short time the wounded gendarme was comfortably established in the town hospital under a false name with all details of accident, etc. in consequence. But the enemy was not far off. It was indispensable both for the security of our own town and for that of another about thirty-five miles away where the HQ of may fighting units was established to get to know the enemy's movements and, if possible its immediate plans. The situation was delicate so we had to have some precisions.

It was about three or four o'clock in the morning, we were tired but the mission had to be accomplished. On the road every precaution was taken: no lights, a moderate speed, eyes ears, arms at the ready. In the village where we had discovered the fate of our unfortunate comrades we stopped. Night was fading.

Dawn would soon break and it was the enemy's favourite hour. We decided to try to have some news and after awakening the postmaster we rang up the next village which was only a few miles from German headquarters. Someone replied and after polite replies to a few unimportant questions told us that the road was clear. The Germans had returned into the town. We held a council of war. It was necessary to get to know what was going on. Someone had to volunteer to go into town, into the lion's den so to speak, to ascertain the situation. We all put our hands up. The choice fell upon one of the group, a gendarme, because he knew German very well. Although he could not speak the language he understood it perfectly. As he was a civil servant and carried the official identity card he would not be molested as quickly as another because of the German's respect of all that was military or official. Our plans were to "buy" him a bicycle in the next village, to escort him as near the town as possible where he was to hide until morning and come back in the evening to find him again. But it was written that we were never able to put our plan into execution. In spite of our precautions we ran like schoolboys into an enemy ambush. We had been tricked by the telephone. The road twisted like a serpent along the sloping sides and between the hills.

One of our men, the same as had brought Bob and me to the look-out post, was scouting in front on his heavy motorcycle. Not being used to our tactics of having an armed pillion rider behind him he preferred to go on alone. As there were few crossroads he was quite a distance in front of us. Suddenly, at a turning, we received a heavy burst of gunfire. I was in the second car beside the driver enarming a Bren-gun which protruded from the windscreen. The encounter passed with lightening rapidity. Bullets spattered all around us but we seemed to have charmed lives. Nearly all our windows flew around us in splinters. A bullet came up between the driver and myself but happily touched neither of us while the engine kept running. With the exception of the driver we were all crouched down in the car. With one hand and as accurately as the circumstances permitted I emptied a charger towards the overhanging wood in the direction whence seemed to come the firing. All this passed in a few seconds. Our chauffeurs, who lived up to their reputation of Paris taxi drivers saved us from destruction. To try to burst through was sheer suicide because we were nearing German headquarters. There was safety only in retreat and we retreated with a vengeance. What followed reminded me of those American gangster films. Both cars reversed at full speed. How we did not fall into all the ditches I do not know but in some way we arrived at a country road which arrived vertically with the main road and there in a few seconds our car and then the other turned. By this time the Germans had been reassembled and we soon heard sounds of active pursuit and the chase had begun. Our knowledge of the roads gave us a decided advantage on the enemy. Two sidecars worried us most because they were very fast and carried three men and a Bren-gun but our tactics soon discouraged them. As the road winded like a serpent they had very little chance of firing with any accuracy. We decided to use this natural shield in an effective way. Not far distant was a very sharp bend with a precipice on the right side and the mountain on the other. With a burst of speed we enlarged the distance between ourselves and our pursuers. In the bend we slowed down a little and threw more than half a dozen grenades on the road where they would not be seen before taking the bend. Another burst of speed and we were clear of the danger zone. We heard a deafening roar and after slowing down found to our relief that our pursuers were no longer in sight. On we raced eager to warn the town of the approaching column. Very soon we arrived and broke the news to HQ. We were no little surprised at one item: the enemy had not followed us very far so we began telephoning to one or two of the small post offices along the line. Each gave the all clear except the village where we had left our two dead comrades. They informed us that the column had branched off in direction of the highest mountain in the region. This move certainly meant disaster for one of our camps near the mountain. It was impossible to warn them. The nearest telephone passed through the county's main town which was methodically occupied by Germans and militia. It was a little late to warn them but we decided to do our very best. Our reserves of petrol had run out and as we were undertaking a hazardous mission and had no idea of how, when or where it would end we needed to be forearmed. We had not eaten since the night before so while volunteers were preparing the cars we made a hasty meal, verified our arms and munitions and in a short time were ready to set out again. In spite of our fatigue we had to try to do something for our friends. We could make no definite plans but circumstances would show us how to be most useful. Our motorcyclist companion was still absent and we were worried about him but we hoped against hope that he had broken through the ambush. One of two of our group had small marks on their faces because of flying glass splinters but no serious casualties.

Quite cheerfully in spite of everything we took to the road again intent on making no mistakes this time. Making good speed, totally on the "qui vive" we left the town. A few miles out we distinctly heard the sound of a vehicle. As the countryside was almost uninhabited except for scattered farms sound travelled far in the hills and valleys. We immediately stopped and having sheltered our cars in a cart track we took up position in the bracken. If it was a very heavy column we were to let it pass because our position was of no use for an ambush. If on the contrary the enemy was not in force we were to attack the end of it, do as much damage as possible and scatter. The rallying point was our HQ about fifteen miles away in the mountains. We were scarcely in position when from a bend, doing full speed, shout out a motorcycle. We all shouted together and simultaneously left our cover. It was our friend. He was tired, weary and dishevelled but pulled up with a smile. Our apparition had given him quite a fright but he was so pleased to see us. The joy was reciprocal. In a few words he explained how he owed his life to the speed of his vehicle, to the fact that the enemy seemed to be expecting a stronger "maquis" force and also to the hurry they seemed to be in to go elsewhere. He had been fired upon and chased but had taken side paths into the woods. There he had abandoned his motorcycle in the undergrowth and had hidden in a tree but he had not been followed very far. After staying in hiding a certain time he had scouted around and seeing the road clear had made for home at top speed. In turn we explained how we had escaped and in a few words told him our new mission. He insisted on coming with us and in spite of our protestations took the lead again. The enemy had taken the mountain road so we followed them. The nearer we came to the maquis camp, which was certainly the enemy's objective, the more cautious we had to be. Soon we heard the sounds of the combat. The firing was heavy but spasmodic. It was time to leave the main road. We left our cars behind a farmstead after concealing them as well as possible with straw lent by an obliging farmer. We had followed the mountain road. It had been raining heavily and we found ourselves in a heavy mist which grew thicker and thicker as we went up. We were in a dangerous position and we knew it but somewhere around some of our comrades in arms required our help so on we went. We were risking being shot by friend and foe.

We had not gone very far when one of the chauffeurs who held the lead (we were marching in Indian file on the side of the road nearest the precipice) suddenly stopped and ordered us to likewise. We soon understood why. Standing motionless we were in a few seconds confronted by two shadows which emerged from the steep fall. We waited until they had hoisted themselves on to the road and, arms levelled in their direction, challenged them. On hearing our voices they calmly said, "De Gaulle." When on our summons to step forward they proved to be maquisards we guessed that the worst had happened. In a few words one of them told us the whole story: the mist, German strategy and French treachery had all beaten them. The enemy had sent empty trucks down the mountain road while the Alpine infantry led by French traitors had followed the mountain paths. The movements of the column we had followed had been unknown and the camp had been attacked from the low side. French mobile reserve troops in German pay had taken the way of the grassy slopes and the result was a combined encircling attack. The "maquisards" might have been able to do something or at least make a fighting retreat had it not been for the heavy mist which, joined to the complicity of the attack, made any coordinated action impossible. Actually the enemy was "cleaning up" the stragglers. As far as our new companions had seen there was a great number of dead and a good few wounded but the prospects of saving them were very poor because the principal attackers were German SS, the most terrible brutes who ever donned a uniform. Our only hope of saving some of the wounded was to await the end of the battle and search the battlefield. We decided to do this and had not long to wait. Enemy action had been fast and decisive. Their work done they did not seem to enjoy the prospect of remaining too long in the mountain with a mist which was growing denser every hour and rendering more and more dangerous an unusually perilous road strewn by rocks and often by small avalanches from the mountain itself which menaced to throw the unwary traveller over the deep precipice which bordered the road. When the mountain calmed down we began our sorrowful round. All around were dead maquisards but they had died fighting because the enemy must have had severe losses too. We had gone around almost the whole battlefield and had begun to despair of finding any wounded when groans brought us towards a great mass of rock which must have fallen from the mountain and the road into the valley. Behind it we found two men, one apparently unconscious and the other not far from it. A few drops of "eau-de-vie" brought life back to them, one regained complete consciousness while the other began to cough which action brought a trickle of blood from his mouth.

Our wounded companion who had regained consciousness explained what had happened. His friend and himself had been wounded together. He had had a bullet in the leg while his companion had received a bullet in the abdomen. Seeing the SS "finishing off" certain wounded the first had, under cover of the mist and with great difficulty because of his broken leg, brought his companion to the hiding place where we had found them. After giving them all the care we could we brought them to our cars on improvised stretchers and in about an hour they were in hospital where, later on, they both recovered.

Next day we had further news of enemy movements in the district. Sabotage groups were organised in each direction but there were still a few weak spots where we could not really count upon peasant patriotism to allow the existence of a look-out post. It was essential that these points should be covered by frequent scouting because FFI units if they were to be useful had to be warned of enemy approach. We organised scouting parties whose work was, in civilian clothes, to see what was going on and to try to have some reliable news as to possible German movements. We all went our way and the result seemed satisfactory. But there was one shadow on our happiness: our motorcyclist friend did not come back for his mission. Later we learned that he had gone too far on his motorcycle (he should have hidden it at a certain place and gone on otherwise) had been arrested by the enemy and shot five miles further on. The next few days were spent in continual missions of sabotage or of liaison between different units and HQs. Only one stronghold was left in our county and it was there that the remnants of the other dispersed camps were to be directed. As the enemy was constantly on the move in the district roads and bridges had to be mined, trees felled, etc. so we were kept busy organising these different works for local "résistance" groups.

On the evening of the fourth day we were on our way after a liaison to a railway goods station not far from our HQ where we had heard tell of an enemy stock of fuel oil when we were sighted by an enemy column which immediately gave chase. The two cars driven by our excellent chauffeurs gave of their best and we were holding our own until we realised that we were being chased into the town where we knew another enemy contingent would be awaiting us. We had to change our direction. The car I was in was in the lead. Our driver never lost his head a second; he left the road, entered a field through an open gate and at top speed, rocking like a ship in a choppy sea, climbed the grassy slope into an extensive wood. The other car followed us at a few seconds interval accompanied by heavy firing from the column which had stopped. We were only ten but were determined to put up a fight. The enemy had dismounted and tried to advance across the field but from an elevated and covered position we could have been able to hold them. But the inevitable happened. Two armoured cars separated themselves from the others and, under cover of their fire, the infantry began to advance. We retreated, not knowing what was going to happen but prepared for every eventuality. The enemy advanced to the edge of the wood but did not seem prepared to go any farther. It was only later that we understood why. Seeing that we had a small breathing space we decided to try to hide our cars. Our chief, who was born in the district, knew a nearby gully and suggested that we should try to pack the cars into it. It was hard work but we managed it and soon the two vehicles were covered by branches and only recognisable at very close quarters. We were still very puzzled by the enemy's silence so we decided to investigate. The result was that we found out that the Germans (about a hundred in number) had encircled the wood. Personally I think they were just as worried about our silence as we were about theirs.

Usually the "maquis" fought, sometimes even stupidly in the face of an overwhelming numeric superiority but here we had retreated after firing only a few rounds. They must have thought that here they were in the presence of an organised force which was trying to entice them into an ambush in the wood. Outside of their brutality and systematic disregard for human life the Germans were good soldiers and excellent fighting men but they were wholly unprepared for the guerrilla warfare especially of the kind the "maquis" could have continually waged had they been properly organised and commanded. I have watched enemy columns go through the mountains and on every face I could read anxiety. Heads were turning all the time, soldiers were fidgeting and in every attitude one could see uneasiness. I remember distinctly a German prisoner's summing up of the situation. In very bad French he said: "The "maquis" attacks "here" but when you try to retaliate they are "there". It is impossible to know where they are and where to find them in that place." Had it not been for French treachery and the lack of patriotism among many joined to the lack of cohesion and co-operation caused by greed and degraded personal interest the enemy could have been chased out of France in about half the time. Where was the fault? We shall try to see it at the end of the "recit".

We had retreated to the summit of the thicket and there in a small natural crater we took our stand. We were scantily armed so we decided to await nightfall and try to break through. The day dragged on monotonously. We had neither food nor water. Every now and then we heard movements in the wood but no nothing. The lack of movement began to tell on us. We realised that to stay where we were was simply preposterous and that we were only awaiting certain death. We were worried about our chief who was a member of the famous "Green Plan" sabotage mission. He was not annoyed at the idea of death but as he knew a great number of secrets he feared torture not for itself but for its sometimes drastic consequences because the enemy knew all the pain-making instruments and no matter how courageous a man is he is only a man after all. He had an ampoule of strychnine but would only use it in an emergency. So we decided to split up into twos and to try to break through. The "rendezvous" was HQ. I left with another whose home was in the village where we kept all our stocks. Cautiously and prepared for anything we began to make our way through the wood. Everything went well until we were about half a mile from the open. We had just stepped into a small clearing when we spotted two enemy soldiers who were looking in the opposite direction. Immediately I levelled my Tommy-gun in their direction and would have fired, I could not have missed them at that distance, had not my companion, older and more experienced than me, held my arm. With our eyes fixed on them we waited. In a few seconds they turned. Their gestures were an exact repetition of ours some seconds before. One wished to use his firearm but the other stopped him. In spite of our situation I could not help smiling and my smile proved contagious because the older of the soldiers smiled back. My companion then took a risk which proved a success. Holding his arm in one hand he advanced with his left hand risen in the form of a salute. I followed him, my gun at the ready. The others advanced repeating the salute. He made a sign to the enemy soldiers that they should go one way while he went the other. One of the Germans pointed to one direction, uttered a vehement, "Nein," and pointed another way. We thanked him and pointing in a direction told him that it was the good one. We then parted after a military salute. I kept looking behind me but the enemy kept his word. In spite of their making us understand that they had shown us the safest way we kept a vigilant look-out but they had been honest and we were soon out of the wood and on our way to our mountain lair. When we arrived were soon joined by another two and little by little the whole group was back at home without a loss. The whole operation had lasted ten hours. Only two of our small groups had had to fight their way out of the wood and there had been no accidents on our side. You can quite imagine our joy when we were all together again. After a night's rest we accomplished our mission in spite of all. With two trucks we went to the station which was only three miles from the then German-occupied town and raided a big stock of fuel-oil which was destined for these same troops. The operation was quickly and calmly done thanks to the help and information of the stationmaster and all his employees. It was staged as a hold-up and we all saw to it that there were enough scenes of pillage and disorder to justify this excuse. The enemy command accepted this excuse when they came in the afternoon to collect their belongings. In order to be sure that nothing would happen to those who had once again helped us we were hidden in the bracken on the hill on the other side of the rural station buildings ready to intervene. We could have acted in all liberty because an HQ was not far from the spot and we had plans made to waylay on a signal any vehicle which might be carrying a prisoner. The local resident "résistants" were only too pleased to accept such a mission just as they were of great help for sabotage work in their respective districts.

That evening Bob and I were chosen to go back again to the look-out post which had been our first mission on joining the group. Enemy movements had become very frequent and this post being extremely important had to be perfectly manned. Our chief thought, and later events proved that he was right, that local "résistants" were neither conscientious nor careful enough. We undertook our new mission with mixed feelings because we preferred the rough and tumble active life of the group to this sedentary post but we had to obey. During our previous stay in the village we had made may friends so we cheered up at the thought of not having to go into an unknown place. The peasants seemed to respect us because in all truth we both had a very good education (both of us had been at the university) and they had become proud to invite us to dinner. For those who understand and have lived among these mountain people who with very few exceptions have never left their lonely farm or village this will be no surprise. We had everybody's confidence and were treated even with deference by all. One person above all was very kind to us and we had nearly all our meals in her home. Her husband was in prison in Germany and she had two sons, one about eleven years of age and the other about seventeen. The latter had been in a professional college in one of the important towns of a neighbouring county. As he was on holiday my companion and I had given him a few lessons in mathematics and other subjects during our free time when we had just taken over the post. The facts may seem superfluous but I wish to mention them because of the signal service this lady rendered me. Had it not been for her courage and coolness I would very probably not be alive today and the village would be only a mass of charred ruins, another of many charming souvenirs[4] of German occupation in France. Our first twenty-four hours passed uneventfully. One thing surprised us however and that was the quite considerable number of light "maquis" vehicles which passed on the roads. On telephoning we learned that the enemy had invaded and destroyed the last of our big concentrations in the county. Only another one remained in the region and it was in a neighbouring county. We were given

---

[4] *memories*

no details but it was a great disappointment for everyone.

Next morning everything seemed quiet. HQ warned us of enemy movements all over the district but could give no details so we simply remained on the look-out. At mid-day, my companion went for lunch and when he came back I went in my turn to the home of the lady mentioned above. As the family had already eaten and the boys gone back to look after the cattle on the hillside I was dining alone. The lady was busy with the washing up. I had finished and was just smoking a cigarette when the youngest boy rushed in and shouted, "The Germans are coming!" He had seen them from quite afar on the hillside because of the long winding road. "Go and warn Bob. Tell him not to worry about me," I said to the boy and made for the door. "No you don't," said the lady, "there is no cover here and you would be spotted and killed immediately." She then took my revolver and handed me a pair of old trousers, an unpalatable three-quarter length blouse and an old hat as worn by farmhands. A big pair of "sabots" (wooden shoes filled up with straw to keep them from wounding the feet) and there I was. But the disguise was incomplete. A handful of cinders from the wood fire, my hair away under my hat and I was just one of thc numerous farm hands one finds on the roads near the villages. I had just changed and my uniform had just been hidden when a considerable enemy column thundered into the village and, what was more dangerous, stopped. Ignoring whether we had been betrayed or not I had to leave the house both for my own safety and for that of the village so I gathered us a pitch-fork and another tool used for cleaning out the cattle shelters on the hillside and making a terrible noise with my wooden shoes made my way out of the house. But a surprise was awaiting me: The lady of the house pushed me from behind so that I almost fell on the cobblestones in front of the house and began shouting and swearing at me as only a Frenchwoman can do it. She treated me as one of the laziest, good-for-nothing men she had ever seen and warned me that if I had not the shelters cleaned out by the evening she would fire me. In my whole life I never felt so embarrassed but her stratagem worked like a miracle. To take the mountain path I had to cross the road between the German trucks. The soldiers all laughed at me. Those who understood French explained what was happening and I took the road to safety amid their scoffs and jeers. Near the top I met Bob who was hiding behind a dry-stone wall. As I could afford to do it I began pottering about near a corral and from there much relieved to see the column moving off again. Only a few officers and men had dismounted. They seemed to have carried off a few big cheeses from the village dairy where they were made daily. We both breathed a sigh of relief because we were afraid that they might have discovered the telephone wires (Bob had hidden the telephone itself) and have sacked the village. After this experience we decided to keep our telephone hidden and as much as possible to take position on the heights from which we had an excellent view for miles around. Later we were pleased to have this position. The inhabitants of the village were delighted with our decision because they had had quite a scare. We were more than thankful to these simple-minded people and in particular to the prisoner's wife who had risked keeping my uniform and revolver in her house. She had put herself in a very dangerous position for our safety not only in hiding my belongings but also for entertaining us regularly at mealtimes. Had there been any real trouble through discovery of our telephone system or of my uniform it is more than probable that certain of the inhabitants to spare their own family and belongings would have put the whole blame on this woman who was acting so patriotically. Her fate and that of her family and belongings would have been that of so many hundreds who had helped the "résistance": firing squad or deportation with confiscation and utter demolition of all her belongings. Knowing this we appreciated all the more her "beau geste" but at the same time we understood the ordinary peasant's attitude although we would not always approve of it. But the farmers had other reasons for not liking the "maquis". Marauding bands wearing "maquis" armbands without ever having devoted a day of their lives to any "résistance" work went around the country forcing the peasants under the menace of firearms to give them eggs, bacon, cheese, fat, butter which they brought into the towns to sell at black market prices. In its spare time our group hunted down these robbers.

There were also others on the road coming from attacked and disbanded camps (certain camps counted two to four thousand men) who after a certain time spent in the woods found themselves penniless without food and far from home in an unknown district. They were trying to find their way home in groups. The main roads were infested with enemy columns. Very often the towns or localities they came from were occupied. These poor young men had to live. Whenever the people were charitable enough their subsistence was assured but very often the peasants either became tired of the continual stream of needy persons or seeing their reserves low could do nothing to help. In these cases the inevitable happened and the "maquisards" became robbers. What a pity to think that these young and ardent men who had left their homes in the hope of being able to do something for their country should end thus. Had the movement been better and more practically organised it would have been more useful and have left a better souvenir[5] in the country. Later when speaking of the tactical changes operated in the organisation I shall give my personal ideas of how I think the resources of men and war material could have been more effectively used. All these reflections were brought home to us that evening by the arrival in the village of ten of the survivors of the last considerable camp in the county. There remained only the other important concentration of "résistance" troops in the region and it was soon to follow the example of the three others.

That evening I was taking the first watch on the hilltop. Everything seemed quiet when I suddenly heard the sound of a rolling stone. Someone was

---

[5] *memory*

coming up the mountain path! I retreated behind a dry-stone wall and, my finger on the trigger of my Tommy-gun, I waited. Soon Bob's voice called my name. I replied softly but did not relax because I realised that he was far from being alone. In a very short time, having left his companions behind him, he was beside me. Ten men coming from the big camp which had been scattered by the Germans had come into the village shortly after nightfall. They had asked for permission to sleep in the barn. The peasant had accorded it and immediately afterwards have come to warn Bob who had spoken to them and verified the truth of their statements. We were determined to help them to the best of our ability. I found that there were ten of them. They were literally exhausted having marched across country during two whole nights and the first part of this one. Their first needs were food and sleep. Bob went down to the village accompanied by three of the younger members of the group to see what he could find in the way of food and clean straw which would serve as bedding in one of the cattle shelters. During their absence I left two of the young men at my post showing them the roads and asking them to call for me if anything unusual should pass or happen on them while I brought the oldest member of the little group and his other companions to a shelter not far off. I explained to him that as he knew his comrades better than I did and as they seemed to obey his orders that he would have to take charge of them. I assured him that we would explain the situation to our chief as soon as possible and then he would certainly find a solution to the problem. In the meantime we would arrange everything from a food point of view but that in every way we would have to abide by the chief's decision. In the meantime there must be no plundering. They must stay on the hilltop so as not to alarm or annoy the peasants in any way. The man said he would take all the responsibility and that his companions would do nothing to cause trouble. With this understanding, after visiting the shelter and making our plans, we came back to my post to be rejoined a few minutes later by my friend who brought enough food to last about a day (at least I thought so) and a good deal of fresh, clean straw. Supper was cold but the lads did more than justice to it. I do not think I have ever seen food go so quickly. They must have been simply ravenous. What I thought should have lasted at least twenty-four hours disappeared in about an hour. When they were at last satisfied we were able to ask them a few questions as to the battle which had ended in the camp's dispersion. It was always the same story. Betrayed by their number and by lovers of easy money at any cost they were attacked by an armoured force superior in numbers, military training and tactics. The Germans had even used aircraft against the position. For nearly four hours four aircraft had bombarded, bombed and machine-gunned the camp's outpost. It had been a very bad day for the "maquis" who had had their heaviest losses since the beginning of the campaign. Our men had been more confident on that occasion than many times before because they had, for the first time, light Browning machine-guns. But of what use were these against tanks, armoured cars, light artillery and, above all, light bombing planes. They had also electrical magnetic arms against armoured vehicles but generally they were out of use through lying in the damp grass where their batteries had run down little by little. The men had not been sufficiently instructed in their use and the result was generally speaking catastrophic. Once again I felt that we had before us another result of the lack of organisation in the "maquis". Having explained how lucky they were to have been able to escape from the enemy our new companions gave, each one, their appreciation of the battle. It had been very hard but they were certain that had they been better armed and not betrayed they could have held the enemy but in spite of all they had accounted for a good number of Germans who would certainly not have the joy of seeing their country again. It was really amazing to see the splendid "morale" of these men who in spite of their past and present hardships were still ready to fight. They were tired so after accompanying them to their "hôtel" and assisting them in the making of their "beds" we wished them "Goodnight" and held a "council de guerre". The "Chief" must be warned and asked to take these men to safety for two reasons: their own good and the post's security because their presence on the hill might alarm certain peasants who often came to see about their cattle and they might report the fact to the inhabitants who fearing for their own security might do something rash which would prove disastrous for the post. Next morning after giving details of the new situation created by our new arrivals we were told to keep them hidden and in safety for the next twenty-four hours when something could be arranged for them. We felt quite satisfied but remained faced with one big and important problem, food. The night before we had had an example of their colossal appetites. We could not think of asking the villagers to feed twelve of us. They would certainly have done so gladly but we did not wish to be a burden to them in any way. There was only one solution: go to the nearest little town, about four miles away, and try to find what we needed. If we had any surplus we would share it among our benefactors in the village who, in spite of their relative abundance, were sometimes short of certain things and, above all, of sugar. So we decided to take this step and as I was older than Bob, the Germans were always very suspicious about young men, I decided to go. Our plans were quickly made. I borrowed an old pair of trousers, wooden shoes, a cowherd's "blouse" (which hangs loosely almost down to the knees) and an old greasy hat. A small donkey and cart completed the disguise. If asked for my papers I would have no difficulty because although my identity card had been established in another county I had taken care through a friendly gendarme to have my change of address made for the village where the post had been established. In case of accident I slipped my colt into my belt and off I went imitating as well as possible the cowherd's slouching gait. I took to the main road and for about a mile all went well. Then I spotted the unmistakable brown and cream of enemy vehicles. The countryside rolled up and down in regular hollows but was a bare as a billiard table. No hope of escape in case of emergency so I decided in case of questioning and perhaps searching to get rid, temporarily, of my revolver. Cautiously I pretended to be looking after my donkey and, taking note of where I was putting it, I let my colt fall into the grass-covered ditch at the side of the road. It took only a second but I have scarcely accomplished my act when the column was upon me. The motorcycles and first light cars passed on. So did the twelve trucks. I began to breathe more freely when the last light car of the whole column stopped and a young officer stepped out. "Papers?" said he in perfect French. After fumbling about in order to play my part of soft country bumpkin I presented my identity card which, as I said before, carried my change of address which was dated from the beginning of the month of May. With my head bent I waited for my possible questions. I had not long to wait. "Why did you leave the county you were living in until May?" Speaking as ungrammatically as I could I said, "The "maquis" was forcing everyone to take to the woods there so I left to come here to be able to continue to work and earn money. In the woods you earn nothing and you are always in danger while you have not much to eat. Here I work, earn my living and am sure of my food." "You are a reasonable and careful man," said the officer. "Where are you going to now?" "I am going to the town for provisions for my boss who lives over the hills about five miles back," said I. "You can go," replied the officer and I went with a mumbled, "Thank you," breathing a sigh of relief. The conversation had lasted only a little more than a minute but I was pleased to see the end of it. The car moved off speeding to catch up with the column. I began to fuss around my donkey and once the enemy was out of sight I gathered up my revolver and carried on with my interrupted errand.

On my arrival in the locality I went straight to the mayor's office. I asked to see the mayor himself and soon found myself in the presence of a dapper little gentleman, very intelligent-looking but brief in his manner of speech. In a few words I explained my mission: we were twelve men in the hills (I gave no position). We were without food and could not continually be a burden to the peasants. We were without ration books of any kind. Would he please give me the necessary papers to enable me to purchase what we needed. I had money and was willing to pay. With a wave of his hand he swept my idea aside: he could give me no ration books because he had too few and required them in case of emergency. Communications were too difficult to allow him to send for more. All I could do was trust to luck and go from shop to shop explaining my case. I then asked him to give me at least an official paper carrying his signature which would serve as an introduction to the traders and once more I insisted on our situation telling him that if these men were not fed they might take the law into their own hands. He only shrugged his shoulders. I felt my patience going to pieces as I took my revolver from my belt and putting it down on the edge of the table asked him whether or not he was going to try to help us. If he remained as stubborn I was simply going to help myself. Our case was quite serious and I could not afford to stay in this office for hours. The sight of the firearm seemed to quieten him down. In a moment I had an official paper signed by himself and asking the shops to help the bearer. I thanked him, apologised for having shown my gun. On him seeing the paper I was received with open arms. Few would accept payment and those that did so gave me more than value for my money. I returned home with a sprightly step and on my arrival was made more than welcome because of all I brought back, above all because my comrades had sighted the column and had feared the worst. We had a good feast and were even able to give certain things to our benefactors in the village because we had become used to a rough fare and could do without certain dainties such as sugar and coffee which were very scarce. On calling HQ that evening to give the daily report we were told to stand to the next morning when, circumstances permitting, the chief would take our visitors in charge. True to his word the chief's car accompanied by a light truck arrived at the post towards ten o'clock next morning. He asked the newcomers if they were still willing to continue warfare against the enemy. They replied affirmatively so he explained that the high command for the district had decided to change their tactics and to form small commando groups whose task would be to harass enemy columns and supplies on the highroad. The essential conditions were courage and absolute discipline. He was going to take them to a small camp where there were already ten others. There they would receive further orders. We asked to be allowed to accompany our friends to their new camp and it was with joy that we handed over the duties to two other men from our own group.

The new camp was about twenty miles away in both an advantageous and dangerous position not far from the main road. The woody belt in which the men were to live was long and quite deep. As we had already been warned there were ten men there. They seemed quite comfortable but were evidently suffering from inaction and so were happy to see the others because reinforcements usually meant activity. The road they had to work on was very important because it united the two counties. Supplies seemed plentiful, arms and munitions, in food state and well-chosen for guerrillas. In brief the "Chief's" choice and organisation seemed excellent. After a very good meal the chief, whose duties called him elsewhere, left us promising to be back in the evening with further supplies and a field telephone. About an hour after his departure, approximately 2.30 p.m. the lieutenant in charge of the camp with two of his companions prepared to go to the town situated about three miles away to see the local "résistance" chief. In order to pass the time I asked to be allowed to accompany them. Bob had found an old school friend among the men already in the camp and was very happy to speak with him of old times so I was a little lonely. The three were only too pleased to take me with them and we set out on our short journey in very high spirits. But ill fate awaited us. We were just entering into the town when we fell head on, on a German column. The driver with whom I was sitting in the front seat had just the time to stop and open the door to try to jump out when he received a bullet in the head and lay half in and half out of the car. We were very near the edge of an abandoned square overgrown with high weeds and higher nettles. I slumped out of the car, rolled into the nettles, crawled as I had never done before and have never done since and soon was in a clump of trees one of which I climbed and hid myself in the branches after throwing the contents of a big packet of pepper (we always carried this through fear of German police dogs) on my tracks. I could see nothing but could not be seen among the heavy leaves. The Germans had now stopped shooting but I could still hear their hated guttural voices quite near the thicket. They then began to fire again and bullets whistled among the trees. It was quite uncomfortable but would have been much more so had they searched all the trees. Why did they not do so? I do not know but the fact is that they came no further. After a certain time I heard the sound of the column moving off again. An hour later I ventured down and a very pitiful sight met my eyes as I looked cautiously above the weeds; a small party of villagers were busy carrying off something in a wide, bullock-drawn cart. After making sure that there were no Germans around I ventured out to see what had really happened. On that simple cart were the bodies of my three companions. The two others had been killed in trying to run towards the cemetery which was on the other side of the abandoned square. They had offered too easy a target and had paid dearly for it. I think that I owe my life to them because of the distraction they thus made. On explaining to the men who were there what had happened I was told that I really owed my life to the fact that the column seemed to be in quite a hurry. I immediately thought of our camp and was really very annoyed to learn that some of the farmers had thought that they had heard shooting not very far away a short time ago. Assailed by fears of every kind I took to the road resolved to rejoin the camp as quickly as possible. Our car had been burned on the square so I had to walk the way back.

I took to the fields following the main road as much as possible but was met about halfway by our men. The camp had been attacked but the column had been spotted before its arrival and the young men, finding themselves without a leader and unorganised had offered scarcely any resistance. Their position had been sold. One of the men had slipped out of the woods a few nights previously and after a few bottles of wine had been too loquacious. He had confessed this when they had had the first news of the enemy's arrival and this had been a big moral factor in the rout. When I told of our mishap and its results the men were disheartened. We told those who came from the district to return home. The ten men we had brought from the post remained with Bob and me and we undertook our long march back to our starting point which we reached in the night. There bad news awaited us. Another enemy column had taken the direction of the town and according to news received seemed to be preparing to stay there at least a day or two. We had a certain amount of provisions but they would not last very long. Our new companions were discouraged. They had been in three camps and each one had been dispersed. We reviewed the situation together. It would not be wise to allow them to set out in the directions of their homes because most of them had quite a distance to go and we had no exact news as to enemy movements. As Bob and I were well known in the village we decided to ask our friends if any of the farmers would agree to take these men until they could find their way home. Next morning we did so and the reply was so favourable that in the evening each one had a temporary home. All of then stayed in farms until the county was cleared of Germans and one even took a permanent job there. Two or three days afterwards we were all four recalled to HQ. The local "résistance" group was to take charge of the post.

Very shortly afterwards I had the narrowest escape of my life. On 9th July there was to be a meeting of the important "résistance" chiefs of the county. The object was the reorganisation of remnants of companies after the dispersion of the county's two big camps. In many localities these men awaited orders and very often were in a precarious position without liaisons, etc. The Allied troops were making progress and there was still work to be done to hinder the passage of enemy troops from the south of France to the north. After twenty-four hours hard work making reports (we preferred fighting to secretarial work) we all met in the town nearest our HQ which was the one directly covered by the look-out post. Towards ten o'clock in the morning everyone was there: the second in command in the county, a lieutenant chief of the local group of the town, two men, René and Georges and two women heads of important groups, our chief, the second in command's chauffeur five members of our group, of which I was. The meeting was more than interesting. Many plans were made for the constitution of mobile groups whose task was to hinder the enemy columns from reaching the north of France and from there Germany. Arms and munitions were to be collected and a vast system of liaison established so that columns could be attacked at precise intervals. The plan was magnificent. According to my ideas this system should have been adopted from the very beginning. Had it been so many lives would have been saved and the "maquis" work would have been much more effective in every way. It was quite easy to understand that a considerable force of men in a wood or a mountain anywhere will certainly attract attention because these men must eat and they cannot live eternally without having to go out now and again for supplies. These gatherings might have remained hidden longer had there not been so many traitors in the country but France was a divided people during this period and in such times one always finds lovers of easy money. The "Maquis armament was totally unsuited for a defence battle against a modern-equipped mechanical army. They should have been an essentially attacking force. As it was these huge camps awaited the German attack which came to each one of them in turn and even if they retreated only after a noble defence in which they accounted for a great number of the enemy they did "effectuer" the work they could have done had they been properly organised. Arms and munitions which, may I say so, were as if not more important than human lives because of the circumstances, were lost in these big battles where the fighting was done by one or two companies while the untrained men often fled in disorder. It was, so to speak, a case of "every man for himself". Some men, even youths who had never been in battle before, did marvels but others, tormented by the thought that here there was no quarter, no prisoners, fled sometimes ignominiously as was the case of the captain I knew, throwing their arms into a wheat field in case they might be found carrying them and be shot in consequence.

The meeting had taken place in one of the back rooms of a hotel near the railway station. Once finished we left the three most important chiefs together for dinner and we went to another part of the hotel where we could relax a little and take part in our own dinner without being under our chief's hawk eye. We were delighted with the meeting. The decisions taken were unanimously approved by us and we were all impatient to see them put into action. The meal was excellent and as we had been told to have the cars ready for 2.00 p.m. we left the dining room towards 1.30 p.m. Our motor car was driven by charcoal gas (this may seem a little strange but it was quite common in France during the occupation). We busied ourselves with the car. I put a leather satchel in which I always carried my British passport and which had been used for the purpose of carrying the chief's papers (happily he still had them with him) in the back seat of the car and went to our secret reserve in the outbuildings of another hotel just opposite the one where we had held our meeting and dined to bring two sacks of charcoal. I had just left the old shed and was coming along the side of the hotel towards the car when one of my friends, looking a little pale, called to me "Jerry is there!" I did not believe him. We had dined very well, the wine had been excellent, news seemed good so our spirits were high. I thought my companion was only joking because we were covered by the look-out post and any enemy movement would have certainly been telephoned to us. But on my arrival at the car I was obliged to give in to the evidence – Jerry was there! Less than eighty yards away in the main street stood a German armoured car. I was saluted by a spray of machine-gun bullets. I immediately dropped by sacks by the car and pulled my revolver. Forms were beginning to appear behind the leading vehicle and bullets began to rain around the car from behind which suddenly appeared one of my friends. "Let's make a fight of it for Maurice! Come on!" Our first impression was that our career had suddenly come to an end. We were really in a tight corner. Fighting in my locality was very dangerous, not so much for us, we were soldiers, as for the inhabitants because we had too often seen the German way of avenging their dead and wounded but we really had no choice. One issue and one only was open to us; try to hold the enemy until a way of escape presented itself. Our only cover was behind the block formed by the small hotel in whose outhouse was our reserve of charcoal.

Had we been able to cross the street we could have reached the open but I doubt if we could have gone very far; the surrounding country was made of innumerable even hillocks used as a grazing ground for cattle. To venture out in open territory was certain death in nine cases out or ten. We decided to make the best of it. I took the corner of the hotel (our car was standing at the corner which was farthest away from the enemy) my friend took the opposite side of the alley (about fourteen feet wide) which separated the hotel and another building. The other three members of the group must have taken the opposite side of the building because we heard shots coming from there. In the shadow of the armoured car Bren-gunners carrying ammunition began to make their way towards us. We were trapped grouped together as we were in such a small space. Our firing, however, seemed to be causing them a great deal of worry because they did not advance as quickly as they really could have. Two of them however, more daring than the others, made a bid for it, passed the first opening beside the hotel and came straight for our country. The constant fire from the armoured car allowed this advance. We were being closed in! My companion and I firing sparingly (I had only two charges for my colt) retreated step by step along the hotel wall. Having counted my shots I knew that half of my ammunition was spent. Feeling my way along I arrived at a door and stepped into it to change my charger. I had no wish to enter the hotel. All I desired was to have time to make my firearm ready for further action. But I had to do without these few seconds' respite. A brutal hand pushed me off the doorstep. It was the proprietor of the hotel. He was afraid that I might want to take shelter and endanger his business. He was quite wrong and I had the chance to explain it to him later. Little by little we were forced to retreat. Behind the building we all met - the five members of our group, Georges, another "marquisard" and the second in command's chauffeur. Bullets were coming in from both sides. The walls of the outhouses became bullet spattered. Our situation was desperate. We felt the enemy closing in on us and decided to make a bid for freedom. We did not know the town very well and had only a very faint idea of our whereabouts in it. Now and again the enemy came round to the back of the hotel and fired straight at us. Once I had to fall flat to avoid being shot down by a Bren-gunner who otherwise could not have missed me. In spite of the circumstances I had to smile. One of my friends, seeing me fall as the soldier fired, swore as I have seldom heard a man do so and cried out "Maurice is dead!" I jumped up again but a few shots had sent the too adventurous enemy to shelter. In a few seconds we made our plans. Our munitions were going fast. We must use all we had, make a little room for possible movement and then make a bid for it. We did so. Our stratagem worked and most of my friends made for a little wall about four to five feet high. I realised that they would have a certain difficulty in all getting over it so I took the back entrance to the hotel, climbed a stairway, heard footsteps behind me and turning, ready to use my last bullet, found Bob behind me. "What are we going to do?" he asked. "Get out of here as quickly as possible" I replied. "Wait here, I am going back down to try to see how the land lies." Having motioned to him to continue his climb to the top storey I began to go downstairs as cautiously as possible. I had only about twenty stairs to go when, looking over the rail, I saw an armed German sentry. Without even taking time to turn round I backed up the stairs. For the time being it was impossible to get out. Hurriedly I rejoined Bob. He was still a little at a loss. I then had a brainwave. We both had regular identity cards, why not use them? Our uniforms would give us away but in a hotel there is always a possibility of hiding them. We both went into a room. In the wardrobe were two suits about our size. All we had to do was dress and wait to see what might happen. We changed, hiding our uniforms in an old trunk but all of a sudden I remembered that my passport was in our car and on that same passport was my photo. If the Germans made a regular search (they were very likely to do so because British papers usually meant Intelligence Service and they were more than afraid of it) I was lost. A British spy would be a great catch for them and it would be useless for me to try to explain my situation. Bob could get out of it without too much difficulty but my case was more serious. It was useless for me to try to leave the hotel. My friend could support a German interrogatory; I could not. We were on the top floor of the hotel. A small staircase which must lead to the attics was before me. I decided to take it. From there I climbed through a skylight on to the roof. I was taking quite a chance but preferred this solution to waiting to be gathered up and shot. The skylight opened out on to the side of the roof opposite to the street. With one hand on the apex of the roof to steady myself (I was wearing heavy army boots) I made my way towards one of the chimneys. I had about six yards to go but I had scarcely done two when a revolver appeared from one side of the above-named chimney. I was trapped. I was certain that my antagonist was one of our own men so I said sharply, "If you shoot me we are both marked." A second later a head appeared around the corner of the bricks. It was the county second in command's chauffeur. "Sorry, old chap, but if it had been a Jerry I would have had him before I went myself. "How is everything going?" "Badly. I think we have three killed. My chief, the lieutenant and your boss have fallen in the open over on the other side of the town. Why in the name of everything did they take to the open? Unless something happens we are done for." "Any bullets left?" "One," I replied. "Well we will go down fighting."

The firing had died down a little when all of a sudden we heard the unmistakable sound of a Bren whose regular fire was punctuated by cries of alarm from the Germans. We risked a peep over the top of the roof and saw them running to cover in the street. Soon only an armoured car was visible and it seemed to be making its way towards the station. Our chance had come so we must not lose it. In a minute or two we had climbed down from the roof. My companion made a break for it. I called Bob and we went downstairs as casually as possible. At the back door I had a look out. No sight of the enemy. I sent Bob through one of the outhouses towards the back of the town. As for myself, I was anxious to know what had happened. There was no sound of firing so I knew Bob had broken through. I strolled out rolling a cigarette, relying on my borrowed clothes to save me. As I arrived at the end of the back of the hotel I met a German soldier, Tommy-gun in hand. It was no use trying to pass him. Near the little wall, the place of the other friends' getaway, was a small place of convenience for gentlemen. I made for it walking as calmly as possible. To give myself a countenance I made the biggest mistake of the day. I only came out of it alive because of the German soldier's stupidity. My cigarette made I put my hand by sheer force of habit in my right trouser pocket and, in doing so uncovered my 45 colt which is not an easily hidden arm. The German saw it. "Achtung!" he shouted. His warning gave me time to put the small lavatory between him and myself. Two leaps and I was on the wall. But the enemy had reacted quickly. I was not yet completely off the wall when at least ten rounds spattered the wall only an inch or two below my body. Small pieces of brick and plaster hit me on the neck and the right hand. But I had jumped without knowing what awaited me on the other side. I fell about ten to twelve feet into an evil-smelling stream (it was the town sewer system). In front of me were numberless gardens while behind me was a tunnel through which flowed the water. My decision was rapidly made. I leapt into it and after wading a few steps bent double I found a very narrow bank on each side and more headroom. I placed myself on one of the banks exactly at the spot where the tunnel suddenly widened out. I had only one bullet but if the enemy came to look for me I might be able to bluff that I had more. I heard the sound of firing above me and smiled. The vegetables in the gardens were being watered with hot lead this afternoon.

Soon everything calmed down. Now and again I heard the sound of stamping feet above me and the guttural voices giving orders. I did not wish to stay too long in my position. Firstly I did not wish to be caught in a trap and secondly the stench was terrific. I had been in the sewers about half an hour and everything seemed to have quietened down when I decided to try my luck. Taking my time I went back down into the stream and began to wade. At the end of the tunnel I surveyed the gardens. There was not a great deal of cover but here and there were patches of uncut hay. The enemy did not seem to be around. Making myself as small as possible I made my way across the gardens. All of a sudden I heard the noise of traffic and saw enemy vehicles on the road which ran parallel to the gardens at a distance of fifty yards. I lay in a cabbage patch, my body as near the ground as I could until the column seemed to have gone.

Then I got up and decided to make my way to a big château a mile off which was the local "résistance" HQ. On my way I was delighted to meet Georges and the two lady members but before catching up with them I knew that something was wrong. They soon explained everything: René was dead. He had met his end in saving our lives. It was his intervention which had allowed us to come off the roof of the hotel and make good our escape. He had broken through the Germans with his car which had been left behind at the hotel in which we dined. At top speed he had made for the most elevated part of the country behind the station and from there, firing above the station roof, had swept the main street with his Bren thus obliging the enemy to withdraw. But he had been helpless against the armoured car which had shot him through the head at short range. He had died fighting and fighting alone a hopeless battle. This news was a great shock to me but it was a stimulant. I was proud to belong to our organisation which counted among its members many heroes. I soon reached the outskirts of the château grounds but caution was necessary and I was soon pleased to have used my head a little. Behind the château the ground swept up into a sharp, thickly wooded climb which ended in a very wide plateau. Instead of going directly into the grounds I skirted them and having arrived on this hill all round the venerable old building a German every two or three yards. There was nothing I could do there so I decided to leave the town and spend the night in some barn or other before coming back to report next morning. Accordingly, taking my bearings as accurately as possible, I began my tramp across the fields my object being to cut across the main road into the neighbouring county, reach the other main road leading to the town, which was our new F.F.I. general headquarters and take the first possible occasion for a rest before coming back to the scene of our recent combat. After walking a certain distance without seeing a single habitation I met an old farmer who explained how I could find my way on to the other road. I had simply to go down a lane, walk about ten yards on the main road, take a cart track to the right and continue as straight as possible across country. In answer to my question he told me that a quite important enemy column had passed on the road about half an hour ago. I immediately changed my plans and headed for the road with the intention of regaining the town as quickly as possible to see if I could do anything. When I arrived on the tarmacadam the only person I saw before me was a young girl but I had scarcely walked three yards when the first vehicles of what proved to be a light enemy column came out of a bend. The thought flashed through my mind that after the engagement in the afternoon the troops would be on the "qui vive" and I remembered that I was still carrying my revolver. I quickened my step, took the young girl in front of me by the arm and, putting my head down close to hers as lovers do, I whispered to her to keep calm and have confidence. If anything happened I would take all responsibility. Walking thus we crossed the road between the two German trucks which were a little separated and took the cart track the old peasant had spoken to me about. The girl was terrified and instinctively tried to turn her head. I begged her to refrain from doing so and soon we had the consolation of hearing the sound of the last truck die away in the distance. The whole event had only lasted one or two minutes but my friend was exhausted. She sat down on the grass at the side of the road almost unable to speak. The strain had been very great. To soothe her nerves I told her how everything had happened and without giving any details explained my nationality and how the loss of my passport had put me in a very serious situation. This seemed to cheer her up and she began to find her colour again. She must have thought I was from the Intelligence Service or something like that and it seemed to please her. I said nothing to take away the possibility of such a mistake and after thanking her wholeheartedly continued on my way. My idea was still to reach the town in case I might be needed.

The first habitations I reached were those of a small hamlet. I dropped casually into one of the homesteads and after some general questions asked news of what had happened in the town. I was told that two men had been killed and another very seriously wounded and was very much relieved to learn that no harm had come to the inhabitants. A few windows had been broken by shots and that was the limit of the damage. On my question as to the nearest telephone I was looked at in a very anxious fashion and told that about a mile farther on was another locality where I could find what I was looking for. Thanking the peasants I continued on my way, hugging the side of the road, ready for any emergency. Soon I reached my goal and had no difficulty in finding the local post office which was also an electrician's shop. On the phone I only said one word, "D'Artagnan." The reply was a guttural exclamation. I immediately hung up the receiver. So the enemy was still there! The fact of my passport being in the lost car made it too dangerous to attempt to enter into the town. I must wait until morning. Perhaps they would leave then. For the time being my only chance was to wait around somewhere because I was worried about my friends. I did not know the country well enough to be able to find my way to HQ without passing through the town. To give anyone the name of the village was by far too dangerous. To rest my legs a little I went to a little café, sat down at a secluded table from which I could see the road and ordered a glass of wine. I had not been long there when a middle-aged man entered, went to the bar, ordered something and after a certain time came over to my table. Begging me to excuse him he began conversing about the weather, etc. I asked me if I was a stranger to the country. While speaking I noticed that he kept looking around him. Suddenly he came to the point. "You hung up rather quickly on the telephone just now." "Did I?" I replied quite calmly. "Was it the presence of the Germans which annoyed you?" "Why? Are the Germans in the town?" He simply stared at me: "You know they are." I saw that he was feeling uneasy and decided to get to the bottom of it. "Have you ever been to Saint André?" I asked suddenly. He immediately smiled and replied, "Yes, round about the Saint John." His hand shot out across the table and caught mine. "Why didn't you speak sooner? I suspected that you were in the "résistance" and realised that you were in a tight corner. I am the local chief. You cannot go much farther because "Jerry" is there. Let me take care of you." I was pleased to meet him. He led me to his home, introduced me to his wife and did everything to make me comfortable. I let him do the talking and after being sure of him explained in a few words the situation. He knew the "chief" and our HQ, having received my orders concerning sabotage work by way of our group. According to his way of thinking it would be unwise to undertake the long trek to HQ (more than fifteen miles). The enemy would certainly not stay long in such a small town (they never had) and he was sure that I would soon be able to communicate with the group. But although I was quite of his opinion I was too worried about my companions and knew that they would be very worried about me to stay there. I decided to wait a little and try again to have a telephone communication. While waiting I partook of a very good meal. My new friends were most hospitable. However my effort was useless. The Germans were still there. By this time it was getting quite late. On my friends' offer I accepted to spend the night with them, determined to leave early next morning. My room was on the first floor and my first care was to open the window and prepare a hasty retreat if anything unforeseen happened. It was my first night in a bed since I left the hospital for the "maquis". The softness of the mattress worried me not a little but I was very tired and soon was sound asleep.

Early next morning I was awakened by my host who told me the enemy column had passed on the road shortly after dawn. After a hasty toilet and breakfast I found a small pony and trap awaiting me. It was raining but I was too impatient to arrive in town to notice it. I was just passing in front of the château gates when one of the local "résistance" boys was arriving on his bicycle. I hailed him and on seeing the look on his face realised that something was wrong. The trap had already stopped when I had jumped from it and ran to meet him. The look-out post had announced another enemy column which would arrive at any minute. There were three young boys lying wounded in the château, two had their legs in plaster so could not walk alone. The day before they had been hidden in a turret because nobody had had any time to take them away but it would be more prudent to take them to a safer place. I ran up the drive behind the cycle, was immediately recognised and told the plans; the wounded were to be evacuated towards a small hamlet about two miles away behind the château. There were only two of us to carry the wounded because the caretaker of the house had to stay there in view of a possible visit. Carrying each one a wounded man on our back we made our way, the young man I had met and myself, towards the hamlet. The going was heavy and I had to stop now and again to help my comrade who, not being very strong, could not keep the pace. However, after a certain time we arrived very tired and pleased to lie down in the straw in a barn to have a rest. After two hours' wait we spotted a cyclist coming down the country road. It was the caretaker coming to announce the "all clear". More slowly this time we made our way back to the "château". There I was able to ask the question which was worrying me. The replies, although not quite as bad an I expected, were bad enough: the second in command of the county had been killed, riddled with machine-gun bullets; the lieutenant, local résistance chief in the town had had a leg shot off and had died from lack of immediate care (the town surgeon had refused through fear to help him in time); René, as I already knew, had been shot through the head. There were no other casualties and no reciprocals had been made. From this last fact I concluded that none of the German soldiers had been touched because usually is cases of casualties during such engagements the ratio was ten or twenty to one for a soldier and fifty or a hundred to one for an officer. The hostages were chosen among the morc important personalities in the agglomeration. But there was little time for reflection. I must get in contact with the group because I was worried about them and knew that this sentiment was reciprocal. From the château I asked for HQ but the local post office, on asking simply if I was a member of the group, informed me that my comrades were in town. They must have been warned of my arrival because two of them met me on my way to the town. What a joy to be together again. The "Chief" had been worried. When during the surprise attack I had fallen to avoid being certainly shot down they had thought that I had been wounded and after the engagement, having had no news of my whereabouts, many supposed that I was dead. This morning the group had come down from the mountains to pay their last tribute to our fallen comrades. The arrival of the enemy column had obliged them to hide but this afternoon they were set on fulfilling their task. In town I met my other friends. All were happy and each told me very simply how he had escaped. One had run the gauntlet of German fire in trying the reach the château to warn them. Another had spent the night in the sewer below the town after being severely shot at. Bob had slept (if sleep was possible) behind a hedge. The "Chief" after posing as dead had succeeded in escaping. Generally speaking I had been more fortunate than any other because I had had a good sleep in a real bed. But we must bring our fallen comrades honourably to their last resting place. The enemy was too much in movement to leave them. If any SS troops happened to pass their bodies were liable to be burned by them. With all due ceremony we transported them from the hillside through the town to the cemetery. The small procession was viewed with mixed feelings by the inhabitants. More than once we were obliged to ask certain individuals to uncover their heads in respect. This annoyed us very much. After the ceremony the "Chief" called a public meeting. He explained the reason for the surprise attack. The look-out post had been unmanned by local "résistance" members. Why did they not warn the town of the enemy's arrival? An enquiry was to be made. If it was a case of desertion a meet punishment was necessary: three men had been killed and the town put in danger of destruction. The result of the enquiry was that the two young men in question, finding the post too quiet and fastidious, had gone off to a dance about two miles away. The enemy had passed while they were amusing themselves. Sounds of the engagement coming up from the valley had given them an idea of the results of their neglect. They had disappeared and were only found later when the occupying enemy had left the district. Their hardships and remorse were judged by the local authorities to have paid for their neglect but they did not bring our dead comrades back to life nor would they have rebuilt the town had burned as considerable villages had already been for less.

The next few days were spent in carrying orders from one group to another in execution of our late superior's orders. Nine days later we received the order to bring to our HQ a depot of five tons of arms and munitions which had been hidden in a wood by the "résistance" near the town where a short time before three of my companions had been killed while I escaped. We had only an approximate idea of the place in the wood but we had to go quickly because the enemy had been informed of the "cache" and we were to outdistance them. Accordingly we set out - two motorcycles, a private car and a huge, yellow ten-ton removal van. We arrived at the wood which fringed the main road about midnight. After posting two Brens, one at each extremity of our area, we set to work. The depot was found in a clump of thickly branched pines at about a hundred yards from the road. We began to carry the containers to the van but it was very slow and tedious work. The moon was full and our presence was visible from quite a distance. In the wood every sound seemed magnified; every word had its echo. We decided to try a more rapid solution, went to the nearest farmstead, woke the farmer and explained that we wanted the loan of a small cart and a pair of oxen. He consented willingly on the condition that he could accompany them. We explained exactly what we were about to do but he seemed only more willing to help us. Thanks to this help we had soon finished our work and after trying to reward the farmer (he would accept nothing) we speedily and without incident arrived home. But a big surprise was in store for us. Next morning, shortly after dawn, we were awakened by the "Chief". He had just been warned by telephone that a rapid German column of considerable importance had taken the direction of the railway station just below our HQ. The enemy might have learned the whereabouts of our position. If surprised we could scatter and hide in the numerous shepherds' huts in the mountain but we must remove all traces of arms and munitions from the village and, above all, empty the removals van which was hidden at the low end of the double range of little country houses. Immediately we set to work transferring them to a little abandoned dry-stone shelter in the slope below the village. We formed a chain. It was hard work but was soon to become much harder. Work had only been going on about half an hour when a little shepherd boy came hurrying up to us breathless. The column had taken the country road and was examining the hamlets (comprising three or four homesteads) on the way. Now the road had the form of an S with our village on a small track at the extremity of the last bend. We had to work fast. The "Chief" gave the boy his field glasses asking him to keep a watch on the beginning of the top bend of the S. Soon he came to tell us he could make out the enemy vehicles in the last little hamlet. What was more serious was the fact that he thought he could see soldiers on the height (this last hamlet was above ours) using field glasses. The "Chief" verified his statement. The boy was only too correct. We must work cautiously and rapidly. I never worked before as I did then. Half crouching, half scampering we at least succeeded in clearing all evidence of our presence. The most important part of the removal van's engine was taken away and telling the villagers to say that is was simply an old, abandoned vehicle (they helped us to make it appear so) we scattered. But we were never to know why the enemy did not visit our HQ. Our precautions however proved to the inhabitants that we did not wish to cause them any worry and resulted in our winning their friendship more than ever.

The region's food situation was precarious. Since D day the enemy had forbidden all vehicular circulation on the roads. All vehicles were to be fired upon without warning. Later doctors' cars and food transport lorries were tolerated on condition that the former flew a very visible red cross and the latter an even more visible white flag. However as carburants of every kind were exceedingly scarce and as circulation by rail was monopolised by the occupation force, food and especially flour was very scarce. It was often well-nigh impossible to procure a piece of bread. Because of this we were pleased to learn that in the town near the wood where we had taken the arms and munitions the night before was a stock of flour belonging to the enemy. We decided to lose no time in raiding it. At nightfall we were ready to set out. Our formation consisted of ten men with two motorcycles, a fast car and a five-ton truck. The operation was successful and rapidly carried out. After an uneventful journey we arrived in the locality and went straight to the place where the flour was hidden. We were quite astonished to find the little town in complete darkness and strangely quiet. Even the guardian of the "depot", who had himself informed the “résistance” of the quantity and whereabouts of the precious cereal did not reply to our first two summonses. When at last he did open the door he seemed more than surprised. “I thought that they were back again.” were his first words. The reason for his surprise was that the enemy had left the town only a quarter of an hour before our arrival. We had arrived at a quarter past eleven and they had left at eleven o’clock. Had we taken the other direction we would have had to fight with a considerable, heavy column. Our work was quickly done. We left proofs of our visit so that the Germans would have no reason to annoy the baker and were soon back in the big barn among the hay pleased to rest a little after those hectic twenty-four hours.

During the days which followed we were very busy distributing the arms and munitions among the different groups and continuing the perfection of the new organisation of scattered forces. We all began to feel that now we would do something really worthwhile. On 23rd July, three days after the flour raid we received a message that what appeared to be a liaison officer alone on a motorcycle and sidecar had been sighted. Three of us were sent out to capture him, if such is the correct expression. We found the vehicle outside a farmhouse and the officer seated before the fire having some refreshment. He offered no resistance and followed us like a child. We were a little afraid of a trap but soon learned that our captive was a White Russian who had deserted and was endeavouring to rejoin his French "maîtresse" in a town about thirty or forty miles on the other side of our HQ. Our prisoner drove the motorcycle with one of the group behind him while I sat in the sidecar. It was quite a joke to see people running away on our approach and we were lucky not to be shot at on our way home. The "catch" was quite worthwhile: one prisoner, a motorcycle and sidecar with a reserve of carburant, one revolver, two Tommy-guns and five hand grenades.

A few days later I was quite surprised when the "Chief" called another member of the group, a lieutenant and myself and taking us apart from the others explained rather briefly that he had a very important mission in view for us if we would accept it. He had personal reasons for not carrying it out himself. When we had declared our wish to do anything that might be useful he thanked us and without further ceremony gave orders for a car to be prepared. On the way he explained the situation: The chief command had asked him to take over the police of the town which had become the region's "résistance" centre. It was a rather delicate task, quite dangerous because of an important enemy stronghold thirty or forty miles away. We were to be under the orders of a major who commanded the entire region. Our work was to keep the town clear of fifth-columnists, guard all the approaches, in general assure the town against all danger from without and within and carry messages to the outposts. To enable us to fulfil our task we had a detachment of fifty F.F.I. under orders of their lieutenant. The local "gendarmerie" was at our disposition. Everything had to be organised. We took over a college and there tried to teach our men a little badly-needed military discipline. Little by little the situation became brighter. Our armament was very poor: rifles, Tommy-guns, Bren-guns, hand grenades, plastic bombs which we made ourselves and a few land mines brought back from our raid on the five-ton munition depot. Four main centres were to be guarded in a special manner because each one led to an important town occupied by the enemy. These four towns were a constant menace to us. From any one of them in half an hour, day or night, a heavy column could fall upon the town - and what could we put in the field against them? A “barrage” made of two old carts drawn across the road and defended by half a dozen men, poorly clad and suffering from the cold mountain nights, armed with a Bren or two, other small automatic arms, not too much ammunition and with our motorcycle as the sole means of communication with the town. Most of the small post offices were with us so that we could be warned in time of any enemy movement in our direction. In this case we had time to warn the town, hide any compromising documents or firearms, warn our men and put them in hiding until such times as the “all clear” would sound. It would have been preposterous to try to defend the entrance of the town against an enemy always fifty to a hundred times superior from all points of view. Of what use would out two crossed carts, one, or if we were lucky enough, two Brens, two Tommy-guns, a few hand grenades and our two or three mines…?

Happily for us we never had a direct encounter with the enemy. As such engagement would have been disastrous for the town and we were to avoid this as much as possible. All we could do was control entries and exits to arrest militia and Gestapo men in flight. Our days passed in patrols in the town and in liaison missions to groups in the country.

In this way we assisted at many ambushes which always took place in the same way. The position, direction and strength of the enemy unit was signalled to us. If the group had a member near a rural telephone we sent the message through; if not we were dispatched to bring the news. The group then chose a favourable position, preferably a thickly wooded mountainous part where the road was on each side surmounted by a steep slope. On top of this slope on one or other, even sometimes on both, sides the F.F.I. took up position. They allowed the most important part of the column to pass then on a signal, usually an animal or bird's call' they showered upon the remainder everything they had: hand grenades, homemade plastic bombs, magnetic projectiles accompanied by a well-nourished fire from all the arms they had. These attacks were thoroughly devastating in spite of their short duration. What was left of the soldiers in the trucks had scarcely time to leap to earth and take up position than the "maquis" was nowhere to be found.

Shortly before France's "liberation" the enemy columns in our region were treated in this manner every five or ten miles of their journey from the south of France to the north. Had this manner of guerrilla warfare been used from the very beginning (i.e. from D day at least) the "maquis"' work would have been more efficacious in every way and the list of casualties much shorter. This would certainly have necessitated another organisation much more centralised but would have given better results in every way. Arms and munitions which were the blood of the "maquis" were lost by tons when the big camps were attacked. The depots were taken by the enemy and the countryside was strewn with those abandoned in flight. Great quantities of food bought by money sent from Britain and North Africa and taken from meagre country reserves were lost in the same way. And these losses were of small importance compared to the loss of life in a hopeless battle of position against an enemy who had everything in his favour to force a victory.

A centralised military organisation would have been a definite advantage in another way because it would have hindered the political division, basic cause of the sterility of many efforts. From the outset the "résistance" movement was divided into two camps: F.T.P.F. (Partisans or Communists) and A.S. (Secret Army or Non-Communists. These two blocks were subdivided, the former less than the latter, but this whole activity was dominated by their respective political tendencies. For example, all members of the F.T.P.F. were obligatorily enrolled in the Communist Party. Although it may seem paradoxical, the "Partisans" labelled themselves anti-militarists and had very few, if any, really qualified officers in their ranks. Personally I have seen young men in the very early twenties who had never had a week's official military training wearing a major's insignia and conducting operations. I remember very well an incident of this kind. It took place in the centre of France in a county renowned as a partisan stronghold. About a hundred Germans were closed up in one of the main towns. They had been asked to surrender and while awaiting negotiations had retired fully armed into a schoolhouse surrounded by a six-foot stone wall. Instead of awaiting the issue of their talks with the mayor, a young partisan officer led a small group of thirty young men to storm the schoolhouse. It is not difficult to imagine the result. The one hundred trained soldiers in this small fort soon turned the exploit into a disaster. Such an operation necessitated other tactics.

The "Partisans" were more numerous than the A.S. and received more arms and munitions than their colleagues. On 14th July 1944 they received a parachutage of ninety tons of material not far from our HQ. The number of aircraft used made us think of the airborne landing we had been promised to often. But one thing must be said and that is that this organisation was really the first to function and accomplish really active work. From the onset the real risks were taken by these men, on the whole ordinary workers. They accomplished their task in the obscurity and danger of the occupation, at the mercy of denunciation prompted by greed or personal vengeance. Their names swell the lists of those dead among concentration camp horrors or ignominiously shot at the roadside. When the BBC encouraged young men not to go to Germany to work these heroes organised small towns in the heart of the country or in the woods where they would await the time of going into action. How many Jews and hunted persons have their organisation to thank not only for their lives but also for their daily bread. It would be well-nigh impossible to give even the approximate number of false identity cards and ration books obtained to succour those in need. All this they accomplished not only under the enemy's eyes but also under those of the government who tracked them down relentlessly because the Communists were then public enemy number one. I do not in any way share their political opinions but justice requires that their efforts and accomplishments be recognised.

The A.S., or Secret Army, was essentially another organisation. Their plan was the establishment in secret of an army regularly hierarchised which was ready for D-day or whenever needed. They received at regular intervals instructions by radio during emissions from London or Algiers. They certainly took part in the organisation of "maquis" camps for those who did not wish to work in Germany but not on the same scale as the "Partisans". The principle members of the A.S. were reserve officers who gave the movement a certain authority. Generally they recognised only one chief, General de Gaulle.

When these two camps found themselves in the presence of one another there was an inevitable clash. The "Partisans" had held the field openly for two, three or four years. They had come to look upon themselves as the sole masters of the "résistance" movement. Suddenly, a short time before D-day, this new organisation came to light led by officers whose ranks were above discussion and whose diplomas, records and civil situation gave them an overwhelming influence. Mass mobilisation plans were frustrated by the new arrivals who brought with them pre-organised groups. These new chiefs had, so to speak, kept themselves in the dark awaiting the favourable moment to appear while "Partisan" chiefs had been carried off by hundreds to concentration camps or shot for their activities. While the other F.T.P.F. leading members had been obliged to leave their houses and live in the woods or on lonely farms these newcomers had all been able to continue their various lives. Some of them were in business and had been more or less obliged to trade with the enemy. On the other hand the A.S. chiefs had personal ideas with regard to military organisation. Their superior education and training enabled them to see the situation in a more practical light than their predecessors who had not been blessed with these advantages. All these facts separated these two important groups and rendered them hostile to one another. However, with a little reciprocal goodwill these difficulties could have been surmounted had it not been for a fundamental obstacle inherent in the French character and particularly inviting to a soldier, who looked upon the "résistance" as the instrument of liberation of the country it should have been, and that obstacle was, in a word, "politics". Political discussions and ideas seem to be as necessary to the Frenchman as the air he breathes. His ideal seems to be to become an active member of a political party on any rung of the political ladder from local councillor to MP. Each underground chief, let him be local, county or regional, seemed to be bent on preparing and assuring his future political situation. They all seemed to be watching one another like cat and mouse, always afraid that one could gain more influence than another. One met with this even among the smaller groups. I remember very distinctly several operations which because of personal antipathy or jealousy among leaders were partly unsuccessful. Early in August we were detailed to organise an ambush in a neighbouring county. The nature of the county gave us every advantage and, I am sure, had the operation been carried out according to plan it would have been a complete success. We received news that an important enemy unit was on its way to rejoin another prior to attempting a journey north in an effort not to be cut off. The junction was not to be allowed to take place and plans had been drawn up for the destruction of the other column. We were to attack in a lonely spot five miles from the nearest town where the road twisted up the side of a steep mountain. The enemy had on his left a sheer drop of about a hundred feet into a narrow valley divided by a river and on his right a high wall of solid rock. Our position on the other side of this deep but narrow valley was unassailable. The range was about a hundred and twenty yards and we were protected by a heavy thicket. We disposed of three sections of about thirty men each. Our armament comprising a few light machine-guns, Brens and Thompsons, although far from being ideal for the French the operation could have proved very efficient because the enemy had no protection in his bare and open part of the road. Above the enemy's head small sabotage groups awaited the moment to blow huge blocks of rock on the different sections of the unit. Our three sections were placed within a space of two miles. Each section was to take charge of about thirty vehicles and choose them at the end of the columns. Everything should have passed off without the least hindrance but we had not counted on political and military rivalry. Because of his education and experience an A.S. captain had been chosen to plan and command the operation. We were in partisan territory and were two groups F.T.P.T. and one A.S. The result was that each officer thinking that he knew better than the other and, above all, the partisan officers refrain to act under Secret Army orders, the plan was not carried out and the operation completely disorganised. The first group attacked the head of the column thus giving the alarm to those behind and soon our positions were receiving an avalanche of mortar and machine-gun fire. The sabotage groups instead of obeying orders blew down a large boulder on to the road in front of the arriving column creating only a very temporary obstacle soon blown into the valley by enemy explosives. Instead of being a perfect success with very little risk the undertaking was, thanks to these military and political differences, a great disappointment.

The same factors were the cause of the "résistance" in our region wasting one of the first occasions they had of wiping out one of the most important combined German and Militia convoy I have ever seen. It was also in August. The Allies were breaking through everywhere and if they were not to be hopelessly cut off they had to leave their headquarters in the chief town of the county we were in and try to rejoin the fighting forces further north. Their only practicable way ran through a very mountainous region most favourable for an attack. At one part of the road they had to go through a tunnel about two miles long. On either side of this tunnel the road was sheer cliff on one side and on the other precipice. About two miles from the tunnel at a very bad bend on the sinuous road was a small but very important bridge. The plans were to attack the convoy comprising three to four hundred vehicles at different intervals, always taking the end as target; when it arrived at the tunnel to let it go into it then blow down both ends, thus closing in a great part. If any passed through this deathtrap they were to meet a road strewn with fallen pine trees and a blown-up bridge. All the while the convoy would be under fire from the hill above. Logically few should have survived. As this was a quite important operation groups were called from all over the district. Here again discussions and petty differences joined to the lack of military experience rendered the operation inefficacious and almost turned it into a disaster for us. The column was prematurely attacked and in the wrong place, this giving the alarm, and from assailants we became assailed because a part of the column closed in on us from behind. At the tunnel only the exit was blown down and, as the mine had not been sufficiently well placed, instead of being completely blocked, the orifice was only partly obstructed. The tanks were able to pass and their weight soon made a passage for the trucks. Bombs and cannons soon cleared the pine logs from the road. The bridge, which should have definitely stopped the column, was only blown up about two feet in the middle. The enemy used the pine trees we had felled to make an arch and were soon on their way again. During this operation we inflicted quite severe losses on the enemy but they were small compared with what they might have been had the different units accepted orders from different officers.

This mutual mistrust went sometimes very far. Each movement had its little "Intelligence Service" which worked not only to know the details of enemy movements and plans but also those of each other organisation. I remember one day in August (I was on my motorcycle with my fiancée, who is now my wife and my best "maquis" souvenir[6], en route to her home) being stopped by a "partisan" lieutenant who

---

[6] *memory*

knew my real nationality and my political neutrality. He asked if I could have any details about a certain A.S. major who had been given a very influential position and whom the "partisans" would have liked to have been able to discredit in order to have one of their own men in his place. This same lieutenant warned me during my stay in the A.S. centre of plans which had been made by the F.T.P.F. to surround the town, disarm all the A.S. groups and take everything over for themselves. Happily they did not carry out these plans because it would have meant a great deal of useless bloodshed but they had their revenge in another and perhaps more efficacious manner. As they saw the danger of losing their influence they created a huge political movement which from its foundation until at least a year after the liberation continued to extend its influential sphere. This movement they called the National Front (a souvenir[7] of the Popular Front of 1936). What they were in danger of losing by lack of personal prestige they gained by numerical strength. All the Communist and left-wing tendencies grouped themselves together in this block. Soon the partisan vehicles instead of carrying the sign F.T.P.F. were

---

[7] *memory*

owned by the letters F.H. (Front National). The Secret Army was divided into several political movements. Seeing the growing power of the left-wing movement a certain number of these, afraid of being unable to share in the political spoils after the liberation, joined the F.N. and so contributed to making it all-powerful. I do not know whether this powerful movement still exists under the same name but I am sure that it had a great part in the shaping of France's post-war political atmosphere.

These considerations, cause of the "résistance's" lack of success in many cases answer part of the question many people asked themselves after the war: "Why did Général de Gaulle not succeed in taking and keeping the head of the country for which he had suffered and sacrificed so much (he had been degraded and even condemned to death during his absence) and fought so hard?"

Like so many countries who had suffered during the war France became more and more democratic. This people of ideologists so easily stirred by well-sounding and glamourous, even sometimes empty words had been the witness of the left-wing heroism. The men who had done so much for this country while tracked like beasts by both their own countrymen and the enemy had earned for their party a rich halo which this imaginative and sensitive people could not refuse them. Many had fought and schemed by their side and had returned to civil life fired by the ideas for which they had fought, suffered and died. The doctrines were extreme but life had enticed many to accept them. Acute food shortage with a necessary recourse to black-market at prices above any working man's means had done nothing to soften a man's extremist instincts. Only people of means could really manage to live and because of this fact they were hated. It may seem difficult to understand this but those who have both witnessed and experienced this situation can comprehend it perfectly. In Marseilles 1941-1942 it was well-nigh impossible to go out without meeting at least one or two funerals and among them many small while coffins. Personally I have known several children who died through lack of milk. To experience these facts embitters but when they are exploited they produce great effect.

Certain older families allowed themselves to be blinded by two things: devotion to their country and fear of communism. These two sentiments led them to activities which caused them to be classed among the most hated of the country's enemies: the collaborationists. For these people Pétain was France's saviour, his word was law, while the Communists were the country's greatest danger and had to be destroyed. The "maquis" and the résistance" in general was for them a lawless band and a danger to the country. I remember very well going to visit a Catholic priest, member of a very old family. As I am a Catholic my desire was to profit from the sacraments during a lull in our activity. It was quite a risk because I was armed and in uniform and had to walk four miles on a very dangerous road. When I saw the priest and explained the reason for my presence I was very badly received and treated as a "bandit and highwayman, a danger to the country". How many religious ministers have I heard preaching and condemning the "résistance" from the pulpit on a Sunday? It would be unjust to generalise these facts. Many of the older families worked hard for the liberation of their country and many religious ministers shared the life and risks of the "maquis". However, a few facts often suffice to make a case. The faults of certain individuals make people forget the qualities and sacrifices of others and a political orator knows how to use everything for his own cause.

Entering into such an atmosphere Général de Gaulle's love of his country was too great for him to stay at its head because, as an old soldier, veteran of 1914-1918, 1939-1940, "maquisard" of the 1944-1945 campaign, said to me, "de Gaulle was prepared to fight against the whole world for France but he refused to fight against the French." In the peace of his retreat he may well be consoled by the souvenir[8] of thousands of members of the "résistance" and of the "maquis" who died with a smile on their lips after throwing to the enemy the cry they had learned to fear, "Vive de Gaulle!"

---

[8] *memory*

La Fin

Available worldwide online
and from all good bookstores

---

www.mtp.agency

@mtp_agency

www.facebook.com/mtp.agency

Michael Terence
Publishing

Printed in Great Britain
by Amazon

63081124R00129